アメリカ人が語る
アメリカが隠しておきたい
日本の歴史

マックス・フォン・シュラー

AN AMERICAN SPEAKS

THE JAPANESE HISTORY THAT SOME WANT HIDDEN

MAX VON SCHULER

ハート出版

Introduction
はじめに

I am different. When you read about Japan and the Pacific War in English, you will find much deep criticism of Japan. You will find statements like "mainline historians agree Japan coerced 200,000 Korean sex slaves".

大東亜戦争や日本について書かれた洋書を読むと、日本に対して批判的なものばかりが目につきます。よくこんな文章を見かけます。「主な歴史学者は、日本が20万人もの朝鮮人女性を強制的に性奴隷にしたと考えている」

But I am different. Why? Well nearly all of these English language historians are Americans. And they use present day America as the standard for the world. What they really mean that America is the most perfect society in the world.

しかし、私はそう思いません。なぜなら、そういう歴史学者は、ほとんどがアメリカ人だからです。彼らは自分たちの国が世界で一番優れた社会だと思っており、現代のアメリカ社会を世界標準のモノサシと捉えています。

If your country is different now, or was different before, it is wrong, and must be corrected. So that is why so many Western historians, mostly American, criticize Japan about the Comfort Women system.

もしも今、あなたの国がアメリカと違っているなら、あるいは過去のあなたの国が今のアメリカと違っているなら、それはよくない、正さなければならない、と思っています。そういう理由で、多くの

はじめに

西洋人の歴史家、といってもそのほとんどはアメリカ人ですが、日本の慰安婦システムを批判します。

But the difference with me is even though I was born in America, I never thought it was the perfect society. Since childhood, I have always thought that Americans boast rather than work hard.

私はアメリカで生まれましたが、彼らと違って、アメリカが世界一優れた国だとは思っていません。私は子供の頃から、アメリカ人は一生懸命仕事するよりも、自慢することに熱心なように見えました。

Americans expect special treatment as a reward for simply being American.

アメリカ人は自分がアメリカ人に生まれたというだけで、特別扱いされるのを当たり前だと考えています。

Also, I have lived my life outside America. If you are a historian, teaching at a university in America, you dare not violate current social customs, such as Political Correctness.

今アメリカの大学で教えている歴史学者は、たとえばポリティカル・コレクトネス(政治的に公正・中立で、なおかつ差別・偏見を防ぐ目的の表現)をはじめとする現代のアメリカ社会の考え方に反する言動はできません。

American Feminists have declared that the Comfort Women system was sexual slavery, and that today's Japanese people must bear guilt for this. If an American historian wrote something different than this belief, he would be forced to lose his job in current America. Feminists would apply pressure to his university until that historian quit.

アメリカのフェミニストたちは、慰安婦は性奴隷であり、今の日

Introduction

本人はそのことについて罪の意識を持つべきである、と断言しています。もしアメリカの歴史学者がこの考え方と違うことを書けば、職を失います。フェミニストたちはその歴史学者が所属する大学に対して、彼が辞めるまで圧力をかけます。

I am not employed by any institution, so I write from a neutral standpoint. Many Americans would say that I have been brainwashed by Japan, since I have lived in Japan so long.

私は人生の大半をアメリカの外で送ってきました。私はどの学校にも雇われていないので、中立の立場で意見を述べることができます。多くのアメリカ人は、私は長く日本に住んでいるせいで、日本に洗脳されたのだろう、と揶揄します。

I fail to see how living in Japan for 42 years, and learning the Japanese language well enough to write books in Japanese, is brainwashing. I think perhaps I have learned something.

私は42年間、日本に住み、日本語で本を書けるぐらい日本語を学びましたが、それが洗脳だとは思えません。私は、おそらく勉強になったと考えています。

And when mainline historians accuse Japan of sexual slavery, American society was not so fantastic during the war. Just look at the situation of Black people, or the status of American women at the time.

主な歴史学者は、日本には性奴隷システムがあったと非難しますが、戦時中のアメリカの社会はそれほど素晴らしいものではありませんでした。当時の黒人の置かれていた状況や、女性の地位を見れば分かります。

Japan is different, and took a different course. And in my opinion a superior course. The Japanese Comfort Women System was the best system ever in my opinion for solving the prostitution problem outside

はじめに

military bases.

　日本は、アメリカとは違う道を歩んできました。私は日本の方が素晴らしい道を歩んできたと考えます。基地の周辺で行われている売春にまつわる問題を解決するには、日本の慰安婦システムは実によく考えた方法だったと思います。

Today's Americans like to pretend that their soldiers will not patronize prostitutes for moral reasons. This is not true, but scenes outside US bases around the world are often lawless and dangerous.

　今のアメリカ人は、道徳的な理由で、自国の兵士は売春婦を買うようなことはしない、と思いたいようです。しかし、それは事実ではありません。世界中のアメリカ軍基地の周辺はたいてい、不法で危険な状態にあります。

Also, I will make some strong criticisms of Korea and the problems of the Japan/Korea relationship. This is not hate speech. It is my deep hope that Koreans can solve their problems in their society without constantly blaming Japan.

　この本ではまた、日韓問題で韓国を強く批判していますが、これはヘイトスピーチではありません。私が心から願っているのは、韓国人は、もう日本のせいにするのはやめて、自分たちの社会の問題を自分たちで解決できるようになってほしい、ということです。

If one tells a truth, it is not hate speech.

　真実を語ること、それはヘイトスピーチではありません。

マックス・フォン・シュラー

Contents
もくじ

Introduction
はじめに／ 2

Chapter 1　Was Japan an aggressor nation?
日本は攻撃的な国だったのでしょうか？／ 12

What war means to Japanese people
日本における "戦争" …………………………………………12

Traditional Japanese post war conduct
日本における戦後統治…………………………………………14

The truth of the Russo/Japanese war
日露戦争の真実…………………………………………………15

Too many Japanese think America can do no wrong
アメリカを信じすぎる日本人 …………………………………17

The American way of propaganda
アメリカによるプロパガンダ…………………………………20

American atrocities
アメリカによる残虐行為………………………………………22

Naive Japanese who do not defend their country
自国を擁護しない愚かな日本人 ………………………………25

The aggressive nature of White countries
白人国家の攻撃的な性質………………………………………26

The true meaning of colonialism
植民地の本当の意味……………………………………………30

The truth of the Japanese/German/Italian alliance
日独伊三国同盟の真実…………………………………………34

もくじ

The true story of how the Japanese/American war started
日米開戦の真実……………………………………………39

Chapter 2 　Were the Japanese Imperial Army and Navy brutal?
日本陸海軍は本当に残虐だったのでしょうか？／ 42

Americans cannot comprehend Japanese people
日本人を理解できないアメリカ…………………………42

Some of my Marine Corps experiences
海兵隊での体験……………………………………………47

Americans will never admit that their troops commit atrocities
米兵の残虐行為を決して認めないアメリカ……………51

Arrogant self centered Americans
傲慢で自己中心的なアメリカ人…………………………53

American troops rape
米兵によるレイプ犯罪……………………………………55

Americans today continue to hide the truth of the war
アメリカが隠し続ける戦争の真実………………………57

The truth of the Nanking incident
南京事件の真相……………………………………………63

How America evaded responsibility for the slaughter of the battle of Manila
マニラ事件はアメリカの責任転嫁………………………66

Do not be fooled by American propaganda
アメリカのプロパガンダに騙されるな…………………69

Many Japanese do not respect their military
自国の軍隊を尊敬できない日本人………………………71

Chapter 3 　The East Asia Co-Prosperity sphere
大東亜共栄圏／ 73

Europe and America feared the East Asia Co-Prosperity sphere
欧米にとって脅威だった大東亜共栄圏…………………73

The true nature of the East Asia Co-Prosperity sphere
大東亜共栄圏の真実………………………………………77

Contents

Chapter 4　Why can't the Japan/Korea problem be solved?
日韓関係はなぜ修復できないのでしょうか？／ 80

The cause of all the trouble is Korea
トラブルの原因は常に韓国……………………………………80

Korean history
韓国の歴史………………………………………………………81

Japanese History
日本の歴史………………………………………………………82

The Yi dynasty class system
李氏朝鮮の身分制度……………………………………………83

Literacy and culture in Yi dynasty Korea
李氏朝鮮の文化と識字率………………………………………86

The Nobles who ruined the country
国を滅ぼした両班………………………………………………88

Contrasting Yi dynasty Korea to the vibrant Edo era of Japan
李氏朝鮮と対照的だった江戸文化……………………………91

The true reasons for the annexation of Korea
朝鮮併合の真実…………………………………………………93

The first Sino-Japanese war
日清戦争…………………………………………………………95

The end stage of the Yi dynasty
末期状態だった李氏朝鮮………………………………………98

The Russo-Japanese war
日露戦争………………………………………………………100

Chapter 5　The truth of the annexation period
併合時代の真実／ 103

Examining documents of the annexation period
併合当時の資料を読む………………………………………103

In the field of Law
法律……………………………………………………………106

The police system
警察制度………………………………………………………108

Finance
財務·····111

Education
教育·····112

Medical services
医療·····116

Agriculture
農業·····118

Japan builds Korea's entire modern infrastructure
日本が朝鮮のインフラを整えた·····121

Chapter 6　The present reality of Japanese／Korean relations
日韓問題の現実／ 122

The most peaceful and prosperous time in Korean history
歴史上最も平和で豊かだった時代·····122

Japan subdued Korea's guerillas
朝鮮人ゲリラを抑えた日本·····123

The Korean victimhood syndrome
韓国人の被害者意識·····127

The Korean superiority complex
韓国人の優越感·····129

Examining the Comfort women issue
慰安婦問題を検証する·····132

Korean prostitutes and US troops
米兵と韓国人売春婦·····134

The truth of the Comfort Women issue
慰安婦問題の真実·····137

Did Japan destroy Korea's culture?
日本は本当に朝鮮の文化を破壊したのか？·····142

The adoption of Japanese names
創氏改名の真実·····145

The Koreans claim that they are the source of Japanese culture
韓国人による文化・起源の主張·····146

Contents

Rampant persecutions in the name of patriotism
「愛国無罪」の暴走 ……………………………………148

Korean actions have blowback
韓国人の自業自得……………………………………149

The Korean poop fetish
韓国人の「大便フェチ」 ……………………………152

The Korean cult of bashing Japan
韓国人の日本バッシング……………………………154

Anti Japanese Korean education
韓国における反日教育………………………………157

"Korean fatigue" among foreigners
外国人の「韓国疲れ」 ………………………………160

Personal memories of Korea
韓国に対する私の思い………………………………162

Korea should learn from Vietnam
韓国はベトナムに学べ………………………………164

Chapter 7　Misconceptions
思い違い／ 170

A naive peacenik and masochistic view of history
平和ボケと自虐史観……………………………………170

American misconceptions about the Japanese/Korean governmental agreement
日韓合意とアメリカの思い違い…………………………180

Blindfolded Americans
目隠しをしているアメリカ人……………………………186

The enduring hatred of the American Civil War
いまだにくすぶる南北戦争……………………………189

North Korea, a master of deceit
欺瞞の国・北朝鮮………………………………………193

What America should strive for
アメリカが目指すべきもの……………………………196

The fantasy of reunification
南北統一の幻想…………………………………………197

もくじ

Korea's true tragedy, the Korean War
コリアの本当の悲劇「朝鮮戦争」………………………204

What Koreans should strive for
韓国人は何を目指すのか？………………………212

Afterward
おわりに／ 214

Notice
注記／ 218

Book List
参考文献／ 219

Chapter 1
Was Japan an aggressor nation?
日本は攻撃的な国だったのでしょうか？

What war means to Japanese people
日本における "戦争"

Many people assume Japan to have been a bad country before WWII, because Japan expanded into other nations. Well, it is not surprising that many foreigners feel this way, after all, they fear Japan.

外国人の多くは、日本は第二次世界大戦の戦中・戦前、他国にまで勢力を拡大したので、日本は悪い国だったと思い込んでいます。これは特別驚くことではありません。彼らは日本を恐れているからこのような考えを持つのです。

But many Japanese also think like this, at least half, maybe more. Why? In America, I would guess the amount of Americans who feel that America is bad for starting wars is less than 10%. And the other 90% of Americans look at them as crazy, naive idiots. Or as potential enemies.

しかし、日本人の半分、いやおそらくそれ以上の日本人までもが、そう思い込んでいるのは不思議でなりません。一方アメリカ人で、アメリカが戦争を起こすのは悪いことだと思っている人はおそらく1割にも満たないでしょう。私は、残りの9割のアメリカ人は、とてもクレイジーで、言いかえると戦争好きな性格を持っているように見えます。

第1章　日本は攻撃的な国だったのでしょうか？

Why is this? Let us consider history. For many years, until the Meiji revolution, Japanese people did not experience war. Now my foreign readers might be surprised at this. But the truth is, Japan did have many wars, but they were basically fought by the warrior class.

　これはどういうことなのか、歴史を見ながらお話ししていきましょう。明治維新までの長い間、日本人は他国との戦争の経験がほとんどありませんでした。この本を読んでいる外国人読者は驚くかもしれません。しかし、実際に、日本では内乱は何度もありましたが、それは主に武士同士の戦いでした。

For the most part, the common people were not involved. Oh to be sure, there were sometimes common people killed in the Japanese mediaeval wars, sometimes towns were burned. These things happen when armies pass through an area. But this was not the goal and intent of the warrior class.

　基本的に、その戦いに一般の民が加わることはありません。もちろん、日本の戦国時代には、時には平民が殺されることも、町が焼かれることもありました。そのようなことは、軍が地方の町を通過する際に起こりましたが、武士が平民や町を襲うことを目的として行軍することはありませんでした。

They fought each other. And for the average citizens there was little effect when a ruler changed. Let us make a historical example. If Japanese were like Europeans or Americans, and thought like them, what about the battle of Sekigahara?

　武士は武士同士で戦います。一般の民にとっては、どちらが勝っても負けてもお城の統治者が変わるだけで、大した影響はありませんでした。具体的に考えてみましょう。もし、日本の武士がヨーロッパ人やアメリカ人と同じような戦い方をしたら、関ヶ原の戦いはどうなったでしょうか？

13

Chapter1 Was Japan an aggressor nation?

Traditional Japanese post war conduct
日本における戦後統治

The Ukita clan, which ruled what has become the present prefecture of Okayama in Western Japan, sided with the Western Armies in that battle. The Western Armies lost to the Eastern Tokugawa forces. After the battle, the Ukita clan was sent into exile, and the Tokugawa appointed the Ikeda clan to rule the former Ukita domain.

　岡山藩、現在の岡山県を統治していた宇喜多家は、関ヶ原の戦いでは西軍に加わりました。西軍が東軍の徳川に負けてしまい、戦いの後、徳川が宇喜多家を岡山藩から追放し、最終的に岡山藩の統治に池田家を任命しました。

The citizens of the area did not resist the change. They accepted it. After all, it really did not affect them all that much. If this had been a European war, the citizens would have been greatly affected. Most men of wealth and social standing would have been put in prison or killed. Property would have been confiscated. Many women would have been raped. People from the Ikeda lands would be in every position of wealth and power.

　統治者が代わっても、岡山藩の民は抵抗することもなく、そのまま受け入れました。結局、統治者が代わることは、民にとって大した影響はなかったということです。ヨーロッパの戦争の場合は、民に大きな影響がありました。富豪や社会的地位がある者は、財産は没収され、牢獄に入れられるか、殺されます。岡山藩の話に置き換えると、全ての富と権力が池田家に集中することになります。

People who had lived in the former Ukita domain would become second or third class people. There would be resistance. It would be answered with massacres. There would be deep hatred between the people of former

14

Ukita domain and the Ikeda clan.

　そして元岡山藩宇喜多家の家臣や領民は、以前より下位の立場に置かれます。すると当然抵抗が起きるでしょう。その抵抗に対する池田家の対応は、虐殺です。そうなると、元宇喜多家の家臣や領民と池田家の間に根深い憎悪の感情が残り続けます。

This did not happen at all. Japanese people simply did not develop such regional hatreds. And the truth is, after the battle of Sekigahara, Japan was ruled by the Tokugawa family, with a military government, and there was no war. For some 263 years.

　日本人は、そのような地域内で憎悪が残る統治をしませんでした。そして実際に、関ヶ原の戦いの後、日本は徳川幕府が権力を持ち支配することで、263年もの間、世界でも稀な戦争のない時代を迎えるのです。

The truth of the Russo/Japanese war
日露戦争の真実

I think many Japanese might feel that the Russian/Japanese war was a mistake, we should have let Russia have Korea.

　多くの日本人は日露戦争が間違いであったと思っているかもしれません。ロシアにそのまま当時の朝鮮を任せれば良かったのではないかと。

No. That would have been suicide for Japan. Why? Because the next target would have been Japan itself. If Japan had not shown the world that it had a strong military, Japan would have been taken by several foreign countries. England, America, France, would have quickly claimed Japanese areas if they thought it could be done.

15

Chapter1 Was Japan an aggressor nation?

　それは違います。それは日本にとって自殺行為です。ロシアが次に狙う国は、間違いなく日本だったからです。もし明治の日本が、あれだけ短期間に強い軍隊を作ることができなかったとしたら、日本はいくつかの国に支配されていたでしょう。英国、アメリカ、フランスは、日本が自国に対抗しうる軍隊を持っていないと分かれば、すぐに日本の領土を差し出せと要求したでしょう。

　Why? This is the nature of foreign countries, especially Western White Christian nations. They must dominate and destroy other countries, and then use for their own profit.

　それは、外国、特に西洋のキリスト教国家の性質だからです。彼らは自分たちの利益のために他国を支配し、その国を破壊しなければならない、と考えています。

A Russian cartoon. A country with the world's largest Army, 4th largest Navy will stomp on upstart Japan.

ロシアの風刺画。世界一の陸軍国、世界第4位の海軍国であるロシアと、新興国日本には圧倒的な力の差があった。

第1章 日本は攻撃的な国だったのでしょうか？

And with America, it is still the same today. European countries have exhausted themselves.

アメリカは、今も変わりません。しかし、ヨーロッパの国々は植民地拡大をやり過ぎて、疲弊してしまいました。

But the fact of the matter is, for virtually all of Japan's long history, Japan did not invade other countries. There was only one exception to this, Toyotomi's invasions of Korea in 1592 and 1598.

ここで注目すべき事実は、日本は長い歴史の中で他国を侵略しなかったということです。例外が一つだけあります。それは、1592年と1597年の豊臣秀吉による朝鮮出兵です。

Many Japanese naively think that Japan was particularly bad, and should exist without a military. Without a Japanese military, South Korea just might invade Tsushima like they did to Takeshima. Koreans are exasperating and annoying, but not yet evil. But in English, there is a saying, "Power abhors a vacuum"

多くの日本人が、日本は特に悪い国だから、軍隊を持たない方が良いという無邪気な考えを持っているようです。日本軍、いや自衛隊がなければ、韓国は竹島と同じように対馬を侵略するでしょう。韓国が特に悪い国だと言いたいわけではありません。英語で「力は真空を嫌う」という諺があります。「力」は「国力」と言っても良いかもしれません。アメリカでは、そういう意味です。弱い国、弱い者がいれば、強い国、強い者に飲み込まれ、支配されます。

Too many Japanese think America can do no wrong
アメリカを信じすぎる日本人

One statement that so many Japanese people make, when I describe the

Chapter1 Was Japan an aggressor nation?

actions of Americans, is that Americans are so nice people, they would never do anything bad.

私は日本人と会話すると、「アメリカ人は優しい人たちで、絶対に悪いことをしない」とよく言われます。

There are several things here. First of all, Americans when first meeting someone, are kind and polite. But it is not true feeling, it is just social graces. In general, Americans do not make deep friendships like Japanese people do.

これには説明が必要です。まず、アメリカ人は初めて会った人には、優しく、丁寧な言葉を使いますが、それは単なる社交辞令です。基本的に、日本人のような深い友好関係を築きません。

And Americans can do very terrible things. Just look around the world. But they think they are doing good.

そして、アメリカ人は非常に恐ろしいことを実行できます。世界中を見てください。でも、アメリカ人は自分たちが世界中で良い行いをしていると思っています。

Americans will always go for their own advantage. There is a Japanese cultural aspect of letting someone else profit at our own expense.

アメリカ人は常に自分の利益になることを選択し、優先します。日本の文化では、自分が損になっても、他人、他社に利益を譲ることがあります。

For example, in a certain industry, there may be five companies. One company may willingly sacrifice it's profit, so that all can flourish. In the future, the other four companies will compensate the one company in some way.

たとえば、ある業界に5社あるとします。一つの会社が、自社の

第 1 章　日本は攻撃的な国だったのでしょうか？

利益を譲歩することで、全社が豊かになるのであれば、その会社は譲歩するでしょう。そして将来的に、その他の 4 社が何とかその譲歩に対してお返しをするでしょう。

There are many Japanese people who think Americans can be dealt with in this way, because they are kind. They think that Americans will some day reciprocate to Japan for Japanese kindness.

アメリカ人は親切で優しいから、日本人と同じように取引ができると考えている日本人が多く、日本が譲歩すればアメリカは将来的に日本にお返しをすると信じているようです。

No, not at all. They may be mystified by the Japanese concession, or think that Japanese are stupid, but they will certainly take the advantage offered. And of course, never reciprocate. They would not see a need to do so.

残念ながら、そんなことはあり得ません。アメリカ人は日本側の譲歩を不思議に思うか、日本人は愚かだと思うでしょうが、譲歩されたその利益は遠慮なくいただくでしょう。もちろん、将来お返しすることはありません。お返しする必要があるとは思いませんし、そんな考えを理解することもできません。

And I think this is part of the reason that so many Japanese people seem ready to believe American propaganda about WWII. They think that because Americans are kind, they would never tell a lie. They cannot comprehend that Americans would use distorted history to press their own advantage.

これが、多くの日本人がアメリカが発する大東亜戦争のプロパガンダを信じてしまう理由の一つだと思います。アメリカ人は親切で優しいから、嘘をつかないと信じているように見えます。こういう日本人は、アメリカ人が自分の利益のために、歴史をねじ曲げて利

Chapter1 Was Japan an aggressor nation?

用するという事実を理解できないようです。

The American way of propaganda
アメリカによるプロパガンダ

Well, they do, all the time. Japan is the only country to ever challenge American world dominance. So America fears Japan. Post war propaganda about WWII has two purposes.

アメリカ人はいつでもそうです。アメリカの世界支配に対して、戦いを挑んだ国は日本だけです。だから、アメリカは日本を恐れているのです。戦後のアメリカのプロパガンダには二つの目的があります。

One to oppress Japan, keep Japan in a perpetual state of guilt. The second is to lie to themselves what about the horrors that America itself committed on Japan.

一つの目的は、日本に圧力をかけ、永遠に罪の意識を持たせようとすることです。もう一つの目的は、アメリカの自国民に嘘を教え、アメリカが、日本に対して行った残虐行為を覆い隠すことです。

This concept of perpetual guilt is the way Americans deal with other people. You can see the same thing in how Americans conduct relations with each other. The problem is, too many Japanese take Japanese cultural nuances and apply them to international relations.

この、永遠に罪の意識を持たせるというやり方は、アメリカ人は他国民に対してよく使います。アメリカ人同士でもやります。問題は、多くの日本人が、自分たちの感覚がそのまま外国に対しても通用すると思っていることです。

There is a deep strain of giving way to others, and assuming that one's own group is bad in Japanese society. As a culture, Japanese people are quick to apologize, even if they have done nothing bad.

日本人はお互いに譲り合い、自分に非があるのではないかと考えることができます。それが奥の深い日本の文化です。日本人は、たとえ自分に非がなくても、円満な関係を維持しようと謝罪をするでしょう。

In Japan, a country that is very crowded, this helps preserve social harmony. But in international relations it is a disaster.

日本は人口密度の高い国なので、このような文化によって社会の調和を維持し、守ります。しかし、外国に対しては、そんな文化は通用しないどころか、大火傷を負いかねません。

Americans, no matter how guilty they are of wrong doing, will always blame some one or something else. That is why in American society you can have murderers who are obviously guilty, say that they are not responsible for that murder. There was something that caused them to do it, perhaps their upbringing by their parents.

アメリカ人は、どんなに間違っていても、明らかに犯罪であっても、他人に責任を転嫁して非難します。ですからアメリカの社会では、殺人犯でさえ自分に責任はない、たとえば自分の両親の育て方が悪かったからだ、などと言います。

A recent case was the "Affluenza" affair. It means that a person grew up in an affluent environment, is spoiled, and is not responsible for their actions. In 2013, in Texas,Ethan Couch, then a teenager, avoided prison with this defense. He was driving drunk, killed 4 people and injured 11 others. Instead of prison, he was ordered to rehabilitation. He and his mother recently went to Mexico to escape rehabilitation, where he was

Chapter1 Was Japan an aggressor nation?

arrested by Mexican police and remanded to the United States.

　最近、アメリカで、「金持ち病」という言葉があります。裕福な環境で育った人は甘やかされていて、自分の犯した過ちに対して、責任をとろうとしない、という意味です。2013 年に、テキサス州でイーサン・カウチ少年が起こした事故を例にあげましょう。彼は酔っ払い運転で、4 人死亡、11 人負傷の大事故を起こしましたが、裁判で、刑務所ではなくリハビリセンターへ行く判決を受けました。しかし、それを逃れるために、母親と共にメキシコへ逃亡したのです。その後メキシコの警察に逮捕され、アメリカへ送還されました。

Americans themselves recognize this, and there is a lot of arguing back and forth in murder trials.

　アメリカ人は責任回避の方法をよく理解していて、殺人事件の裁判でも長い論争を展開して罪を免れようとします。

And this is why keeping Japan in a perpetual state of guilt about the war is useful for America. It takes attention away from what America did.

　大東亜戦争で、日本に対して永遠に罪の意識を持たせるのも、それと同じ理由です。アメリカにとって有益だからです。それでは、あの戦争で、アメリカが実際どのようなことを行ったのか、見ていきましょう。

American atrocities
アメリカによる残虐行為

The bombing of Japan in the war had no military purpose, and the US government understood it at the time. I think it happened because of two reasons. One, the US Navy was really the most useful American military branch in fighting Japan. The Army was not really necessary at all once

22

the Philippines were lost.

　アメリカによる日本への空襲は、軍事的な理由で行われたのではありません。当時、アメリカの指導者たちはそのことを知っていました。私は、空襲は以下の二つの理由で行われたと考えています。一番目の理由は、大東亜戦争で日本と戦う場合、アメリカにとって陸軍よりも海軍の重要性が高かったことです。この戦争で植民地であるフィリピンを失っていたから、陸軍の必要性は当面ありませんでした。

With just Marine infantry divisions, let us increase the number from 6 to 10, the Navy alone could have won the war against Japan. The proper

The city of Osaka was reduced to open fields by B-29 incendiary raids.

B-29による空襲で焼け野原となった大阪市。中央の通りが御堂筋、その右が西横堀川（現阪神高速）と四つ橋筋。

Chapter1 Was Japan an aggressor nation?

strategy was the island hopping strategy, going from island to island, and cutting Japan off from it's resources in the south.

　海兵隊の師団を、6個師団から10個師団に増やせば、米海軍だけでも日本との戦争に勝つことができました。正しい戦略としては島から島への移動、東南アジアから日本への資源供給線を断つことでした。

The Army came up with it's own strategy, which envisioned reconquering the Philippines, and strategic bombing of Japan. But it was superfluous, not needed.

　しかし、当時アメリカでは陸軍と海軍が主に連邦議会において、予算問題で争っていました。特に、太平洋の島で、輸送船が来ると、海軍兵・陸軍兵がどちらが補給物資を貰うかで殴り合いの喧嘩もあったほどです。そこで、陸軍が国会に自分が必要と見せる為に、再びフィリピンに侵攻、併せて日本を空襲する戦略を立てたのです。しかし、この戦略は余計なもので必要ありませんでした。

The second reason was that there were people in America that wanted to exterminate the Japanese people. There still are today. America is very racist and violent country.

　日本本土を空襲した二番目の理由は、アメリカに日本人を絶滅させようと考える人たちがいたことです。現在でもいます。アメリカはとても民族差別の強い、暴力的な国です。

But virtually no Americans will admit this. So if they can keep on forcing apologies from Japan, nobody will look hard at what America did.

　しかし、この事実を認めるアメリカ人はほとんどいません。そして、日本に謝罪を強要し続けていれば、アメリカの行った残虐な行為を誰も知ろうとしなくなります。

第 1 章　日本は攻撃的な国だったのでしょうか？

This may sound strange to many Japanese people, but defending your own country in conversations with foreigners is extremely important.

多くの日本人には不思議に聞こえるかもしれませんが、外国人との会話の中で、自分の国を擁護することはとても大切なことです。

Naive Japanese who do not defend their country
自国を擁護しない愚かな日本人

No one will respect you if you disparage on Japan. They may agree with you, but in their hearts they will think you are mentally ill.

もしあなたが日本人でありながら日本を軽蔑する発言をしたならば、誰もあなたを尊敬しないでしょう。相手はあなたの意見に同意するかもしれませんが、心の中では、あなたのことを頭のおかしい人物であると見なします。

A few years ago, it was August 15th, and after paying my respects to the souls at Yasukuni shrine, I went to a friend's British bar for some drinks. There were two people at the counter. One was a Japanese man, in his 60's. The other was an American, about 45 years old.

数年前の 8 月 15 日でした。靖国神社を参拝してから、英国人の友達がやっているバーへ行った時のことです。カウンター席に二人いました。一人は 60 代の日本人男性、もう一人は 45 歳くらいのアメリカ人男性でした。

The Japanese man kept saying "Oh Japan was so stupid to attack America!" Well the American man, a friend of mine, said, I don't want to hear this! And left.

その日本人男性は「日本がアメリカに攻撃したのは本当に愚かな

25

ことでした」という発言を何度も繰り返していました。そのアメリカ人は私の友達でしたが「そんな話は聞きたくない！」と言って帰りました。

You see, Americans will defend America no matter what. And even if Americans agreed with this Japanese man, they would think of him as feeble minded, and not respect him.

アメリカ人は何が何でもアメリカを擁護します。しかしこの日本人の発言には同意しても、愚かな人物だと見なし、決して彼のことを尊敬しません。

So any Japanese businessman or diplomat who makes bad remarks about Japan to Americans, and tells them that America is a better nation, is not at all thought well of.

アメリカ人に対して日本のビジネスマンや外交官が、日本を軽蔑し、アメリカは日本より良い国だ、という発言したら、アメリカ人はその人のことを信用しません。

Oh, the Americans might use him, but they will easily throw him away.

まあ、アメリカ人はその人を利用するかもしれませんが、利用価値がなくなれば簡単に捨てます。

The aggressive nature of White countries
白人国家の攻撃的な性質

Well, was Japan an aggressive nation? Not nearly as much as America and European colonial powers.

さて、本当に日本は攻撃的な国だったのでしょうか？　植民地を

第1章 日本は攻撃的な国だったのでしょうか？

持っていたヨーロッパやアメリカと日本を比較すると、全然違います。

First of all, how did America force Japan to end it's policy of seclusion? By military force and threat of war. Americans say this was a good thing. Was it? I don't think so. Eventually, with the way events were in the world, Japan would have ended the seclusion policy in it's own way.

まず、アメリカは、どのようにして日本に鎖国政策をやめさせ、開国させたのでしょうか？ それは軍事力を見せつけて恫喝するというものでした。アメリカ人は、それが良いやり方だったと言います。本当でしょうか？ 私はそう思いません。他国に開国を強要されなくても、当時の世界の状況を考えると、日本は鎖国を諦め、開国に向かったと思います。

Commodore Perry's East India Fleet arrives in Uraga Japan, the next year the Japanese/American treaty ending seclusion was completed.

1853年、ペリー提督率いる米海軍東インド艦隊が浦賀に来航、翌年日米和親条約が締結され、日本の鎖国体制は終焉した。

Chapter1 Was Japan an aggressor nation?

But this is indicative of the aggressiveness of White nations, which is now only America. By their nature, they must conquer and dominate. They can not let some nation live alone in peace.

これは白人国家の、現在はアメリカだけの、攻撃的な性質を示しています。他国を征服して、支配するのが彼らの本質です。他国に干渉せず、その国の平和な暮らしを放任するということができません。

Japan's expansion into Korea, Formosa, and Manchuria was of a defensive nature. When Perry's Naval squadron came to Japan, it was quickly apparent to Japanese leaders that if they did not develop a modern Army and Navy, Japan would be destroyed.

日本がその勢力圏を朝鮮、台湾、満洲に拡大したのは、日本を守るためでした。ペリー提督の艦隊が日本に現れると、当時の日本の指導者たちは、近代的な陸海軍を作らなければ、日本は侵略され、滅亡の危機にさらされることをすぐに理解しました。

And to develop modern military forces, industry was necessary. To have industry, you needed raw materials. European powers were creating colonies across the world to ensure their access to raw materials.

近代的な軍を創るには産業は必要です。産業には資源が必要です。ヨーロッパ列強は資源を確保するために、世界中に植民地を作りました。

So for Japan to ensure access to raw materials and national survival, Japan needed to create its own colonies.

そのような情勢で、日本は独立国としての存在を守るために、植民地を作る必要がありました。

The difference is, Japan annexed Korea and Formosa, and developed them into territories of the Empire of equal status with the home islands.

　欧米列強の植民地との違いは、日本は当時台湾と朝鮮を併合しましたが、日本列島と同様にインフラを整え、発展させたことです。

In Manchuria, they created an allied state. Here is where Japan was different from White colonial powers. Those White countries, including America, basically simply exploited the resources of colonized countries. They built little infrastructure, provided little for the populace.

　満洲では、連合国家を作りました。これは、白人国家と全く違う新しいやり方でした。欧米列強は植民地の資源を利用しただけで、インフラを整えることもなく、植民地の住民のためになることはほとんどしませんでした。

Their goal was simply to extract profit. Japan was different. When I first came to Japan, Japanese society was very much more an equal society than America. The emphasis was that all citizens can live at a reasonable level.

　白人国家の目的はただただ利益を絞り取ることでした。日本の目的は違います。私は初めて日本に来た時に、日本はアメリカよりも、はるかに平等な社会でした。ほとんどの国民が、そこそこ満足できる水準の生活を送ることができました。

Americans take another approach. In America, the winner takes everything, the loser does not survive. This is another reason White countries fear and hate Japan.

　アメリカ人はそれとは違う社会を作ります。アメリカでは、勝者が全ての財産を所有し、敗者は生き残れません。これが、白人の国々が日本を憎み、恐れているもう一つの理由です。

Chapter1 Was Japan an aggressor nation?

The true meaning of colonialism
植民地の本当の意味

I have heard that some Japanese people believe America to be a benign nation, and that in Japanese schools, Perry's visit is taught as a polite "door knock". Not at all. It was an explicit military threat.

日本の学校では、アメリカは優しい国で、ペリー提督は礼儀正しく訪問したと教えられているということを聞きました。全然違います。明らかに、軍事力による恫喝でした。

America, like it's ancestral European nations, is an aggressive expansionist nation. America would not let the Indians exist, they were nearly wiped out. Today, only remnants survive. America offered "help" to free the Philippines from Spain. Yet after the short Spanish American war, the Philippine people discovered to their dismay that the meaning of that help was American colonization.

アメリカは、その「先祖の国々」であるヨーロッパと同様、攻撃的で拡張主義的な国です。アメリカの白人たちはアメリカインディアンの存在を許さず、絶滅寸前まで追い込みました。現在、アメリカインディアンは少数しか残っていません。フィリピンに対しては、スペインから独立するための「援助」を提供しました。しかし、米西戦争が短期間で終わると、フィリピン人は、アメリカの言うヘルプは、アメリカの植民地になるという意味だと分かりました。

America certainly intended to dominate Japan for their own profit. It is what Americans do, it is their nature.

アメリカ人は自国の利益のために日本を支配することを考えていました。今も同じ考えであり、それが彼らの本心です。

30

第1章　日本は攻撃的な国だったのでしょうか？

Many people in Japan today still do not understand the true meaning of colonization. What is means is that all the resources of the colonized country are taken from that nation, into the country of the colonizer.

現在、多くの日本人は植民地の本当の意味を理解していません。植民地になるということは、植民地にされた国の資源が、宗主国に全て巻き上げられる、ということです。

In Japan's case, I think we can say that the greatest resource of Japan is the hard working and innovative population. If America had colonized Japan, Japanese people would have worked like slaves for American companies.

Indians massacred at Wounded Knee. They were killed by the American 7th cavalry. The 7th cavalry was decorated for this action.

ウンデット・ニーで起きたインディアン虐殺。虐殺を実行した第7騎兵隊は名誉勲章を授与された。

31

Chapter1 Was Japan an aggressor nation?

　日本の場合、一番大切な資源は、一生懸命働く日本国民です。も
しアメリカが日本を植民地にしたら、日本人は奴隷のようにアメリ
カ企業のために働かされることになるでしょう。

That means a miserable life, with no pleasures, and no freedoms of any kind.

　それは、楽しみも自由もない惨めな人生です。

Americans always talk about spreading freedom, but this is not true. If you really want to understand the truth of this, just look at American society today. The truth is the American way of life has become one of the most miserable among the First World nations.

　アメリカ人はいつも自由な社会という話をしますが、それは真実
ではありません。もし真実を理解したいのならば、現在のアメリカ
社会を見てください。先進国の中で、アメリカの生活が最も惨めな
ものだというのが真実なのです。

European countries, if they had colonized Japan, would have been just as cruel as America. It was the nature of the times.

　もしヨーロッパのどこかの国が日本を植民地にした場合、アメリ
カと変わらない残酷な行為に及んだでしょう。残念ながらそれがそ
の時代の常識でした。

But today, most Europeans have a decent life. In particular, European governments generally provide health care.

　しかし、現在のヨーロッパ人のほとんどはかなり良い生活をして
います。特に、ヨーロッパでは国民健康保険を採用しています。

My ancestral country, the ancient Kingdom of Prussia, had health care. Prussia, being in the center of Europe, could not avoid being caught up in wars that broke out across the continent. So Prussia needed a strong Army to survive. If the population was not healthy, the Army could not be strong. So a State Health Care system was created.

私の先祖の国、プロイセン王国では国民健康保険のようなシステムがありました。プロイセン王国はヨーロッパの中心部にあり、戦争が起こると必ず巻き込まれ、避けることができません。生き残るためには強い陸軍が必要でした。国民が健康でなければ、強い陸軍は作れません。それで、国による健康管理システムが作られたのです。

America has a different approach. It is more important that a few people become extremely wealthy. So the health care system is designed to transfer wealth from the populace to these few individuals. The American people have until recently put up with this system. The reason is because Americans used to believe that every person had the chance to become rich and powerful.

アメリカのやり方は、これとは異なります。数人が大金持ちになることがより重要で、健康保険システムは国民の財産を、その数人に吸い取らせるために作られました。最近まで、アメリカ国民はこのシステムを我慢していました。一般のアメリカ人は、自分が大金持ちや権力者になる可能性があると信じていたからです。

Now they realize that is not possible, and this is the reason for the chaos of the 2016 Presidential election. But the truth is American citizens are not treated well by their own country.

現在、アメリカ国民はその可能性がないことを理解しました。それが、2016年の大統領選の混乱の原因です。そして実際に、アメリカの一般的な国民は、国からまともな社会保障を受けていないのです。

So it is certain that if America had colonized Japan, Japanese people would have been treated horribly.

アメリカは、アメリカ人に対してそうなのですから、もしアメリカが日本を植民地にしていたら、日本人にひどい扱いをしたのは間違いありません。

The concept that Japan was somehow bad for expanding into other countries is simply American propaganda. And the facts are, Japan did not simply exploit other nations, Japan developed them into a status that equaled it's own level.

日本が他国にまで領土を拡張した悪い国であるという考えは、アメリカのプロパガンダに過ぎません。日本は他国をただ開発したのではなく、日本本国と同じレベルに発展させた、というのが真実なのです。

This is unique among colonizing nations, and causes great fear in America. For this reason, Americans have a need to continue to demonize Japan.

これは植民地を有する国々の中では特異なことです。アメリカ人はその日本の特異性をとても恐れています。それで、アメリカ人は永遠に日本を悪魔化しようとするのです。

The truth of the Japanese/German/Italian alliance
日独伊三国同盟の真実

There is another serious reason that Americans regard Japan as an aggressor nation. That is the Tripartite pact between Japan, Nazi Germany, and Italy.

アメリカ人が日本は攻撃的な国であると考える、もう一つの大き

な理由があります。それは、日独伊三国同盟です。

Americans say that Japan allied with Nazi Germany. When Americans say alliance, they think of the WWII alliance between Great Britain and America. There are many photos of Prime Minster Churchill and President Roosevelt in conference, and even joking together.

アメリカ人は、日本はナチスドイツの同盟国だったと言います。アメリカ人が同盟と言う場合、第二次世界大戦の英米同盟を考えます。英国のチャーチル首相とアメリカのルーズベルト大統領が会議中、冗談を言いあっている写真がたくさんあります。

Roosevelt and Churchill in the Atlantic Conference. It was held on the British battleship Prince of Wales, American aid to Britain and the post war world order were discussed.

ルーズベルト大統領とチャーチル首相による大西洋会談。米国が参戦する4ヵ月前に英戦艦プリンス・オブ・ウェールズ艦上で行われたこの会談で、米国の英国に対する軍事支援や戦後の世界構想について話し合われた。

Chapter1 Was Japan an aggressor nation?

Japanese Prime Minister Tojo Hideki never ever met Hitler or Mussolini. Military cooperation between the countries was minimal. If Japan and Germany were truly allies like America and Great Britain, then Japan would have invaded the Soviet Union in Siberia to help Germany in 1941.

日本の東條英機首相はヒットラーやムッソリーニと会ったことがありません。軍事的な協力はほとんどありませんでした。もし日独が米英のような本当の軍事同盟だったとしたら、日本はドイツを支援するために、1941年にシベリアに侵攻したでしょう。

It was not in Japan's interest, so Japan did not. When Tojo Hideki was one of the top generals of the Japanese Imperial Army in Manchuria, he refused Hitler's demand to return Jewish refugees to Europe, and let them settle in Chinese areas under Japanese control. About 20,000 Jewish people survived in this way.

ソ連への侵攻は日本の国益にはならなかったから、日本は攻撃をしませんでした。東條英機は満洲で関東軍の参謀長だった時に、ヒットラーのユダヤ人難民返還の要求を拒否しました。東條英機のおかげで、そのユダヤ人難民は中国の日本軍支配地域で生活できたのです。それによって、約2万人のユダヤ人の命が救われました。

And the Jewish holocaust is the reason for much Japan bashing today. People assume that since Japan and Germany were allies, Japan was as evil as Nazi Germany.

ユダヤ人の大量虐殺は現在のジャパンバッシングの大きな理由になっています。日本とドイツは同盟国でしたから、世界の人々は当然日本もナチスドイツと同じような邪悪な国だと考えます。

The Nazi German holocaust of killing Jews was an awful thing, perhaps one of the most awful horrors of human history. Even today, it haunts people, they cannot make sense of it.

36

第１章　日本は攻撃的な国だったのでしょうか？

ナチスドイツのユダヤ人の大量虐殺は恐ろしいことでした。もしかしたら人類の歴史の中で最もひどいことかもしれません。

But Japan's conduct in the war was in no way comparable to Nazi Germany. In fact, the Imperial Japanese military had more discipline and better conduct towards civilians than most American troops.

しかし、大東亜戦争での日本軍の行動は、ナチスドイツとは比較になりません。実際に、大日本帝国の軍隊は、大多数のアメリカ兵より規律正しく行動し、一般人に対しては特に規律良く接していました。

There is one important aspect that Nazi Germany and Japan did cooperate on though. When Japan attacked the American fleet at Pearl Harbor, an Indian revolutionary, Chandra Bose, was in exile in Germany.

ナチスドイツと日本の協力で、一つ重要なことがあります。日本が真珠湾のアメリカ艦隊を攻撃した時、インド人革命家、チャンドラ・ボースはドイツに亡命中でした。

He took a German submarine to the Indian ocean, where he transferred to a Japanese submarine. He helped form the Indian National Army from captured Indian troops of the British army in Singapore. They fought together with Japan as allies.

彼はドイツの潜水艦でインド洋にやってきて、日本の潜水艦に移乗しました。そして彼はシンガポールで捕虜となっていた英国軍のインド兵たちを集めてインド国民軍を創り、日本の同盟軍として戦いました。

This was an act that was instrumental in achieving Indian independence post war.

これは戦後のインド独立戦争で最も重要なことでした。

Chapter1 Was Japan an aggressor nation?

The only other way in which Japan and Nazi Germany cooperated in the war was the "Monsun Gruppe" or Monsoon flotilla. A few German U-boats operated in the Indian ocean out of Penang, Malaysia.

その他の日本とドイツの軍事協力には、モンスーン戦隊、ドイツ語で「Monsun Gruppe」があります。数隻のドイツ潜水艦が、ペナンの基地を利用して、インド洋で行動していました。

Chandra Bose on the conning tower of the submarine I-29. In the center is the commander of the 14th submarine flotilla, Captain Teraoka Masao.

ペナンに入港した伊号第29潜水艦の艦橋に立つチャンドラ・ボース。中央は第14潜水隊司令寺岡正雄大佐。

第 1 章　日本は攻撃的な国だったのでしょうか？

Japan could supply them with fuel and food, but they could not use Japanese torpedoes. So torpedoes had to be brought from Germany. It was a long journey, and many submarines were sunk on route.

日本からは燃料と食料が供給されましたが、ドイツの潜水艦は日本の魚雷を利用できなかったので、魚雷はドイツから運んできました。長い航海で、途中で多くの潜水艦が撃沈されました。

This was the only joint military action between Germany and Japan in the war. You really can not call that an alliance, in the traditional sense.

日独の軍事協力と呼べるのはこの程度でした。軍事同盟と呼べるほどのものではありません。

Americans ignore good things about General Tojo, like saving Jews.

アメリカ人は、東條英機を高く評価すべき事実、たとえば、ナチスからユダヤ人を救ったという事実を無視しています。

The true story of how the Japanese/American war started
日米開戦の真実

And the facts are that America deliberately provided Japan into attacking America. Any peace negotiation that Japan offered, America refused. And America tracked the Japanese fleet as it approached Pearl Harbor. They let it happen.

そして、日米開戦の真実は、アメリカが、日本がアメリカを攻撃せざるを得ないように仕向けた、ということです。交渉で、日本がどんなに平和的な提案を出しても、アメリカは拒否しました。日本海軍の機動部隊が真珠湾へ向かって進んでいることを、アメリカ海軍の情報部局は察知していました。そして、日本の機動部隊がハワ

39

Chapter1 Was Japan an aggressor nation?

イを攻撃するのを待っていました。

Even when Prime Minister Konoye offered to completely withdraw from China, America turned it down. President Roosevelt and Secretary of Hull expressed some interest in this proposal, but Secretary of War Stimson said that Japan could not be trusted.

近衛文麿首相が中国からの全面撤退を申し出ても、アメリカは拒否しました。ルーズベルト大統領とハル国務長官はその提案に関心を示しましたが、スティムソン陸軍長官が、日本は信頼できる相手ではないと断言しました。

So three and a half years of war and a devastated Japan, was better than negotiated peace? Most Americans today think so. They still think of Japanese people as untrustworthy, as dangerous people, in need of American dominance, to keep them from starting a war again.

その結果、戦争は3年半続き、日本は徹底的に破壊されました。それは、交渉で平和的に解決するより良いことだったでしょうか？
ほとんどのアメリカ人は良いことだったと思っています。ほとんどのアメリカ人の考えでは、日本人は信頼できない危険な国民であり、アメリカが支配していなければ、すぐ戦争を始めると考えています。

This was a very prejudicial view.

これはとても差別的な考え方です。

In annexing Korea and Formosa, and in creating an allied state in Manchuria, Japan was doing what other European countries did.

当時の朝鮮と台湾の併合や満洲国建国で、日本はヨーロッパと同じことをしていました。

第1章　日本は攻撃的な国だったのでしょうか？

Many Americans still castigate Japan today. Why do they not criticize Great Britain or France for killing millions and world expansion? This is simple prejudice.

現在でも多くのアメリカ人は日本を酷評しています。しかし、どうして英国やフランスが何百万もの現地人を殺害して、領土拡張してきたことを非難しないのでしょうか？　これは差別に過ぎません。

Or even America itself. American history is blood drenched. It seems it is impossible for Americans to conduct foreign relations without starting a war.

それから、アメリカは自国の過去も批判しません。アメリカの歴史は血みどろの歴史です。アメリカは戦争を抜きにして、外交を進めることができません。

The problem is, Americans assume that Japanese people are aggressive like they are, thus they constantly assume Japan will attack other countries.

問題は、アメリカ人が、日本人は自分たちと同じような攻撃的な国民なので、日本は他国を攻撃したがっている、とずっと思い込んでいることです。

41

Chapter 2

Were the Japanese Imperial Army and Navy brutal?
日本陸海軍は本当に残虐だったのでしょうか？

Americans cannot comprehend Japanese people
日本人を理解できないアメリカ

I am not an apologist. I am not brainwashed by Japanese people. This is what I hear when I speak with Americans about The Pacific War. They assume that all my years living in Japan has corrupted me. They assume that Japanese people have fed me a constant stream of lies and untruths, and that my 42 years of living in Japan has caused me to forget American truths.

　私は日本の擁護者ではありませんし、日本人に洗脳されているわけでもありません。私がアメリカ人と大東亜戦争の話をすると、こんなことをよく言われます。日本での生活が長すぎて、おかしくなったとか、日本人にいっぱい嘘を吹き込まれたとか、日本で 42 年も生活したせいで、アメリカの真理を忘れてしまったのだ、と。彼らはそう決めてかかってきます。

They assume that America is the center of all truth in the Universe, and nothing useful can be learned in any other country. If I were to try to convince an American by telling them that I am fluent in Japanese, I write books in Japanese, that I have many varied experiences living in Japan, they would dismiss all that as irrelevant.

　アメリカ人は、大宇宙の全ての真理の中心はアメリカであると

第2章　日本陸海軍は本当に残虐だったのでしょうか？

思っています。そしてよその国では有益なものは学べないと考えます。もしアメリカ人に対して、私は日本語が達者で、日本語で本を書き、日本でいろんな経験があると説明し、日本に有益なものがあることを納得させようとしても、アメリカ人はそんなものは関係ないと一蹴するでしょう。

They would insist that what they say is truth, that Japan was a terrible brutal nation, and that a benevolent America modified Japan into a state of semi civilization today. But that Americans must also constantly keep watch on Japan, otherwise Japan would quickly go on a rampage through Asia again.

アメリカ人は、以前日本はとんでもなく残虐な国だったが、優しいアメリカがその日本を半文明国に創りかえてあげた、それが真実である、と主張します。そして、アメリカが日本をよく見張っていないと、再びアジアで暴れ回るだろうと考えています。

Japan's rampage through Asia. This is another phrase I hear again and again from foreigners when I discuss the war in the Pacific with them.

「日本がアジアで暴れ回る」。私は日本以外の国の人と大東亜戦争の話をすると、必ずこの言葉を聞きます。

Part of the problem is that Japanese forces fought to the death, and were extremely disciplined. This terrifies Americans. Well, the truth is, Americans are not really very good at devotion to a cause, especially today.

一つの問題は、日本軍の兵隊はとても統制がとれていて、死ぬまで戦い抜いたことです。アメリカ人はそれに対する恐怖心があります。実際、アメリカ人、特に今のアメリカ人は、何かのために献身的になることができません。

I was a US Marine. We were trained to fight hard, and were trained

43

Chapter2 Were the Japanese Imperial Army and Navy brutal?

to expect that many of us would die in combat. This is unusual for the American military. And many Americans fear the US Marine Corps, and try to destroy us by political attacks.

私は元米海兵隊員です。私たちの訓練は厳しく、戦場で多くの海兵隊員が死ぬことを前提にした訓練を受けていました。アメリカ軍ではこういう訓練は異例です。多くのアメリカ人が海兵隊を恐れ、政治的に潰そうとしています。

Well, for most of American history, Americans have fought in foreign lands. They have had massive firepower, with which they could destroy any enemy.

The American carrier Bunker Hill on fire after a hit by a Kamikaze. Towards the end of the war, many young men volunteered for the Kamikaze Special Attack Corps, even though it meant certain death.

特攻機の攻撃ですでに炎上している空母バンカーヒルに突入中の爆装零戦。戦争末期、死が確実な神風特攻隊に、多くの若者が参加した。

第2章　日本陸海軍は本当に残虐だったのでしょうか？

　アメリカの歴史では、ほとんどの場合アメリカ人は外国で戦っています。どんな相手も圧倒的な火力で粉砕してきました。

Am I saying that Americans lack courage? No. In the American Civil War, the armies of the South time and again beat superior Northern armies in combat. The difference was that the Southerners were defending their homes, the Northerners were invading the South. The Southerners had much more motivation.

　私は、アメリカ人に勇敢な心がないと言いたいのではありません。アメリカの南北戦争では、南軍より北軍の方が兵士の数、武器の質で優れていましたが、何度も南軍が勝ちました。その大きな理由は、南軍にとっては自分の郷土を守る戦いだったのに対し、北軍にとっては南部を侵略する戦いだったからでした。南軍の兵士の方が、はるかに強い危機感を持って戦っていたのです。

But Americans cannot understand the Japanese sense of devotion. So they demonize. They take any incident, and exaggerate it. Whenever they speak of what Japan did, they always add adjectives, like brutal, or uncivilized to the conversation.

　しかし、アメリカ人は日本人の献身的な感覚を理解できないので、日本人を悪魔化します。どんな出来事でもそれを誇張します。日本が行ったことを話す時は常に、「残酷な」とか「野蛮な」といった形容詞をつけます。

Americans are very good at propaganda, at word games. They ignore what their own forces did. A common phrase when referring to American atrocities is, "it was just a few bad apples".

　アメリカ人は言葉のゲーム、プロパガンダの使い方にとても長けています。そして彼らは、自分たちの軍隊が行った悪事は完全に無視します。アメリカ軍による残虐行為について、よく利用されるフ

45

Chapter2 Were the Japanese Imperial Army and Navy brutal?

レーズは、「痛んだリンゴもほんの少しはある」というものです。残虐行為はごく一部の例外、という意味です。

Well, the truth is, war is a horrible affair. In any war, terrible things are done by any countries's armies. Yet Americans will try to convince you that their soldiers were complete angels, while Japanese were awful devils.

本当に、戦争は恐ろしいことです。戦争ではどの国の軍隊でも、大小の違いはあっても、ひどい行為が行われます。しかし、アメリカ人は、アメリカ軍は天使で、日本軍が悪魔であるということを信じこませようとします。

US propaganda about the Pearl Harbor attack.
真珠湾攻撃の卑劣さ、日本人の野蛮さを強調した米国のプロパガンダ・イラスト。

第2章　日本陸海軍は本当に残虐だったのでしょうか？

The fact is, the opposite is basically true. Japanese troops were highly disciplined. In general, Japanese troops behaved well toward civilians.

真実は真逆です。日本軍は規律を守り統制がとれていました。基本的に、一般人に対して規律ある態度で接しました。

Americans on the other hand were not at all disciplined. The Marines and a few elite Army units conducted themselves well with civilians. But the rest of the Army, and in particular support troops, behaved badly. Rape and theft were common.

一方、アメリカ軍は規律を守らず統制がとれていません。海兵隊や一部の陸軍精鋭部隊は一般人に対して規律ある態度で接しましたが、その他の陸軍、特に支援部隊にはひどい者が多く、レイプや強盗は当たり前でした。

Some of my Marine Corps experiences
海兵隊での体験

In my writings, I have written that I was an intelligence agent, that I was never in a shooting battle. Well, actually one time, there was an incident that was somewhat like a shooting battle.

以前の著作で、私は情報部局の人間なので、弾丸が飛び交う戦場には行ったことがない、と書いたことがありますが、一度だけ、銃撃戦の戦場に近い経験をしたことがあります。

I graduated from Marine Corps basic training in 1974. At that time, there was a Left wing people's guerrilla group in California called the Symbionese Liberation Army, or the SLA. Their political goals were obscure, they quickly degenerated into banditry. They were famous for kidnapping Patti Hearst, a newspaper heiress.

47

Chapter2 Were the Japanese Imperial Army and Navy brutal?

　1974 年に海兵隊新兵の基礎訓練が終わりました。当時、カリフォルニア州にシンバイオニーズ解放軍（SLA）という左翼過激派がいました。政治目的がはっきりしないこの組織は、強盗を働くようになり、新聞王ハーストの孫娘、パトリシア・ハースト誘拐事件で有名になりました。

After graduation from Basic training, I was assigned to school in Camp Pendleton California, halfway between San Diego and Los Angeles. When I arrived the school had begun a few days before, and the Marine Corps will always find a way to occupy your free time, so I was assigned to temporary guard duty in an area of Camp Pendleton.

　海兵隊新兵の基礎訓練終了後、カリフォルニア州にある海兵隊の基地、キャンプ・ペンドルトンの学校へ行く命令が下されました。そこは、ロサンゼルスとサンディエゴの中間にあります。私が基地に到着した時は、学校が数日前に始まったところだったので、2 週間待つ必要がありました。海兵隊では兵士に空き時間ができると、その時間を有効に使わせようとします。それで私は、キャンプ・ペンドルトンのある区域の臨時警備を命じられました。

It was an area right on the beach near the main gate. I was often assigned to guard the armory. Most guard stations in that area had only one guard at night, but in the case of the armory, we had two men. Well, that is because the armory is the building where weapons are stored.

　そこはメインゲートの近くにビーチがある所でした。私はよく兵器庫の警備を命じられました。他の場所の場合はたいてい警備兵は 1 人でしたが、兵器庫の場合は 2 人で警備を行いました。兵器が備蓄されている重要な場所だからです。

There was at that time, and probably still is today, quite a trade going on in stolen weapons in America. Various criminal groups would steal them and sell them. Army and National Guard armories were very vulnerable, they only had electronic protection. everybody knew that the Marine Armories were guarded at night by armed guards. However, we were only allowed to carry 5 rounds.

当時、おそらく今もそうだと思いますが、アメリカ国内で、軍から盗まれた武器が闇取引されていました。いろんな犯罪組織が兵器庫から武器を盗んで売りさばいていました。陸軍と州兵の兵器庫は電子警報システムを利用しているだけの脆弱な警備でしたが、海兵隊の兵器庫は夜も武装した警備兵が配置されており、そのことは誰でも知っていました。しかし、私が携帯を許されていたのは、実弾5発だけでした。

Well one night a message came over the radio, there was intelligence that the SLA was going to rob an armory in southern California that night. The guard force on the armory was doubled to 4 men. We were all just out of basic training, and scared.

ある夜、無線で、SLAがカリフォルニア州のどこかの兵器庫から武器を強奪したという連絡が入りました。私が警備している兵器庫に、2人の警備兵が増員され、全部で4人になりました。私たちは4人とも新兵訓練を終えたばかりだったので、恐怖で緊張していました。

On guard duty, there were 3 shifts. The two shifts at rest always slept in their uniforms, they were a reaction force in case of an attack. We would be in bed, somebody would scream "Reactionary!", in 60 seconds, we would be moving in a truck. As we ran to the truck, we were given an armored vest, helmet, rifle and ammunition.

警備任務は、三交代でした。休憩中の二組は、警備が攻撃された場合、応戦部隊となります。それで我々は軍服のままで寝ており、寝ている時に、上官が「応戦部隊！」と叫んだら、60秒以内にトラックに乗り、襲撃された地点に移動することになっていました。ベッ

Chapter2 Were the Japanese Imperial Army and Navy brutal?

ドからトラックまで走りながら、防弾チョッキ、ヘルメット、銃、弾丸を装備しました。

We often drilled this maneuver. Well that night with 4 men at the armory, we noticed the reaction force running outside the fence, drill or a real attack, we did not know. Suddenly, we heard something moving among some wooden crates just outside the armory.

私たちはこの一連の流れをよく訓練しました。ある夜、4人が兵器庫を警備している時に、兵器庫の柵の外を応戦部隊が走っている姿を見ました。訓練なのか本当の攻撃があったのか分かりませんでした。そして突然、私たちが警備している兵器庫近くに積まれた木箱のあたりで、何かが動く音が聞こえました。

The rules were we had to say "Halt" 2 times and then "Halt or I fire!". Then if there was no response, we could shoot. And that meant shoot to kill.

銃の使用に際してはまず「止まれ！」と2回叫び、さらに「止まれ！さもなくば撃つぞ！」と叫びます。それでも止まらなければ、撃って良いことになっています。そしてそれは、射殺することを意味します。

Well, we were scared so we all shouted it out really fast. There was no response, so we 4 Marines all loaded our weapons, and trained them on the crates.

皆は恐怖心でいっぱいで、すぐにその言葉を叫びました。返事がなかったので、私たち4人は実弾が装填された銃を、木箱に向けました。

It was a cat, so of course there was no verbal response. No, we did not shoot the cat, but it was close. But I remember I was very scared, and almost shot that cat. People who have never been in the military, never been in a war, make many judgmental statements about troop conduct. And of course about the Japanese Imperial armed forces.

それは猫でした。もちろん、猫は返事できません。幸い、その猫を撃つことはありませんでしたが、ギリギリのところでした。私が覚えているのは、非常に恐ろしかったことと、危うく猫を撃つところだったということです。軍隊経験のない、戦場へ行ったこともない人が、よく兵士の行動について上から目線で断定的なことを言います。もちろん、日本軍に対しても同様です。

But the fact is, in war, things are very confused, you often end up shooting when you are not sure what is happening. But the truth also is, if you wait to be sure, you could be dead.

しかし、実際の戦場とは、どのような状態なのでしょう。先ほどの猫のように、何かがいて、それが何かはっきり確認できない場合でも、兵士は撃ちます。戦場で、はっきり確認できるまで待っていたら、自分が死ぬことになります。

War is a tragic thing. No, I have not been in a shooting war. But that night, I experienced a little bit of the fear and uncertainty that goes with war.

戦争は悲劇的なことです。私は銃を手に取り、戦場へ行ったことがありません。しかし、その夜、戦争の恐怖と不安を少しだけ経験しました。

Americans will never admit that their troops commit atrocities
米兵の残虐行為を決して認めないアメリカ

But one of the major reasons Americans today keep accusing Japan of brutality is to hide the truth of how badly US troops behaved in the war.

Chapter2 Were the Japanese Imperial Army and Navy brutal?

しかし、アメリカ人が、今も日本兵は残虐だったと非難し続ける一つの理由は、米兵が行ってきた残虐行為を隠すためです。

Americans will never, ever admit that their troops behave badly.

アメリカ人は米軍兵士が行った残虐行為を絶対に認めません。

This is not something that most people know. In fact, the average American thinks that the US military is the most wonderful military in the world.

ほとんどのアメリカ人はその事実を知りません。実際に、一般的なアメリカ人は、米軍が世界で最も素晴らしい軍隊であると思っています。

American troops pose with the skulls of dead Japanese troops.
日本兵の頭蓋骨を集めて記念撮影するアメリカ兵。

第 2 章 日本陸海軍は本当に残虐だったのでしょうか？

But even today, you can read articles in magazines like "The Rolling Stone" how US troops in Iraq rape women and shoot children for fun. They throw candy in the street, when the kids come to pick it up, they shoot.

しかし、「The Rolling Stone」という雑誌の記事に掲載されましたが、現在でもイラクにいる米兵が女性をレイプし、ゲームのように子供を殺しています。キャンディを街の通りに投げて、子供がそれを取りにくると、その子供を撃つのです。

Well, the truth is, Americans make very poor soldiers. There is a certain aspect of the American character, where people think it is good to always question people who are in authority. They think that this is a fantastic thing. They will say that they are not robots, like Japanese people, but free thinking people.

実際のところ、アメリカ人は良い兵士にはなれません。アメリカ人の特徴の一つに、常に権力者を疑うことが良いことで、素晴らしいことだという考えがあります。自分たちは、日本人のように、言われた通りに動くロボットみたいな人間ではなく、自分で意志決定できる素晴らしい人間である、と言います。

But the truth is they are arrogant and obnoxious.

しかし実際は、彼らは傲慢で不快な人たちだ、ということです。

Arrogant self centered Americans
傲慢で自己中心的なアメリカ人

I remember when I worked in a foreign talent office in Japan. We would supply foreign extras and people for Japanese film and TV productions in Japan.

53

Chapter2 Were the Japanese Imperial Army and Navy brutal?

　以前、日本のテレビや映画の撮影現場にエキストラの外国人を派遣する、外国人タレント事務所で働いていた時のことをお話ししましょう。

Most Americans were very difficult to work with. I was a location manager in that company. My job was to be a manager for the foreigners, and translate for them. Often with American people, they would start the day by telling me that they were not going to listen to any instructions from me. They would tell me my job was to translate for them, and to give them what they wanted, like special food, or special rooms to stay in.

　私はロケマネジャーを務めていましたが、アメリカ人は扱いにくい人物がほとんどでした。基本的に、私の仕事はその外国人たちを管理することと、通訳をすることでした。朝集合した時から、私の指示に従わないアメリカ人がいました。その人物は私に、彼らのために通訳と、彼らが望む食べ物や部屋等の用意だけしていればいい、と言ってきました。

They were almost always very arrogant and egotistical. I would try to explain to the Japanese management office, but they would never understand. The problem is, Japanese people think that foreigners will work like Japanese. No.

　たいていのアメリカ人は傲慢で自己中心的でした。そのタレント事務所にそんなことがあったと説明しても、理解されることはありません。問題は、日本人は、外国人も日本人と同じように指示に従って働くと思っていることです。それは違うのです。

In America, people who behaved like that would be fired and sent home, and blacklisted. And that is how you deal with Americans, by threats. The American workplace is a place of tension and conflict, one never knows when he could be fired.

第 2 章　日本陸海軍は本当に残虐だったのでしょうか？

アメリカでは、そんな態度をとる人物は解雇されて、家に帰され、ブラックリストに載せられます。そのような威圧が、アメリカ人と取引、仕事をする際に必要です。アメリカの職場には緊張と対立があります。いつでもすぐ首になる可能性があるのです。

And that is why Americans in business and government are so arrogant and threatening to Japan.

そしてそれが、ビジネスや政府間での取引の際に、アメリカ人が傲慢で、脅迫的な理由です。

American troops rape
米兵によるレイプ犯罪

But in a military situation, it makes for troops who behave like an undisciplined mob. In Okinawa during and after the battle, rapes of Okinawa women by troops was very extensive.

しかし、戦時下において、兵士がそんな態度では、規律のない群衆になります。沖縄では、戦中、そして戦後も、アメリカ兵はたくさんの沖縄の女性をレイプしました。

In the occupation of Japan after the surrender, rapes were common. While the Japanese government was able to provide a prostitution service for US occupation troops, rapes were around 40 per day. But when the US government forced the closure of officially sponsored prostitution facilities, the amount of rapes soared to 330 per day.

戦後の日本占拠期、日本人女性に対する米兵のレイプが、日常的に多数発生していました。日本政府がアメリカ兵向けの売春サービスを提供した期間も、米兵による日本人女性レイプ事件は、一日に約 40 件ありました。しかし、アメリカ政府がその売春サービスを

55

Chapter2 Were the Japanese Imperial Army and Navy brutal?

強制的に中止させると、一日約 330 件に急増したのです。

One incident that particularly upsets me is when three truckloads of US troops arrived at the Omori, Tokyo, maternity hospital, and raped all the female patients and staff. One woman's baby was trampled to death by the Americans. When some of the male staff tried to protect the women, they were killed.

私が特に憤りを感じる事件があります。米兵が乗った3台のトラックが東京の大森にあった産科病院へ向かい、米兵がその病院へ侵入し、大勢の女性患者と女性スタッフをレイプした事件です。この時、入院女性の赤ちゃんが踏み殺され、女性を守ろうとした男性スタッフも殺されました。

US troops line up outside the Yasuura house, a house of prostitution in Yokosuka Japan. To prevent Japanese women from being sexually assaulted by Americans, many such establishments were built.

横須賀の慰安所、安浦ハウスに群がる連合軍将兵。日本人女性に対する強姦を防ぐために、このような進駐軍向けの慰安所が各地に開設された。

第2章　日本陸海軍は本当に残虐だったのでしょうか？

In Europe, American troops behaved the same way. The American Army in France and Germany simply raped and looted as they pleased. Many French people noticed that the German occupation troops in France were more disciplined than the Americans.

ヨーロッパでも、米兵は同様の行為を働きました。フランスやドイツで、アメリカ軍はやりたい放題レイプを繰り返しました。多くのフランス人が、フランス占拠期のドイツ軍の方が、アメリカ軍より規律正しかったと話しています。

Yes, it is true that there was a guerrilla war in France during the German occupation. If, for example, the Maquis, the French guerrillas attacked a German military train, the German Army would go into a nearby village, put all the people in the church, and set the church on fire, killing them.

ドイツ軍の占領下でゲリラ戦があったことは確かです。たとえば、マキというフランスのゲリラ組織がドイツ軍の列車を襲撃したり、ドイツ占領軍がある村へ入り、村人を全員教会に入れ、その教会に火をつけて皆殺しにしたことがありました。

But in basic daily life, the German Army did not bother the French civilians. And for the sexual needs of the troops, the German Army had their own prostitution system.

しかし、日常生活においては、ドイツ占領軍はフランスの一般人を特別構うことはしませんでした。ドイツ軍には自前の売春システムがあり、そこで兵士たちはセックスを処理していました。

Americans today continue to hide the truth of the war
アメリカが隠し続ける戦争の真実

Americans are very good at propaganda, very good at games of words.

Chapter2 Were the Japanese Imperial Army and Navy brutal?

In these days, too many Japanese people are still fooled by American propaganda.

アメリカ人はプロパガンダがとても巧みです。今もアメリカのプロパガンダに騙されている日本人が多過ぎます。

Concerning WWII, Americans say things like, "The Japanese people were deceived by a corrupt leadership". Nowhere do Americans admit that they forced Japan into war.

たとえば大東亜戦争について、アメリカ人は「日本国民は腐敗した指導者たちに騙されていた」と言います。アメリカが日本を戦争に追い込んだ事実を、アメリカ人は絶対に認めません。

The atomic bombings of Hiroshima and Nagasaki are presented as being necessary to cause a crazy Japanese leadership to surrender. Nowhere do they write that the true cause of surrender was the Russian entry into the war. They do not write that the Japanese Imperial Army would have likely repelled an invasion of Kyushu in the fall of 1945, and thus been able to negotiate a peace on terms favorable to Japan.

アメリカでは、広島と長崎への原爆投下は、狂った日本の指導者たちを降伏に追い込むために必要なものだった、とされています。日本が降伏した本当の理由は、ソ連参戦だということは絶対に触れません。また、1945年秋に予定されていたアメリカの九州上陸作戦は、日本軍が米軍を撃退した可能性が高く、その時点で日本が納得する条件を出せば、日本は降伏したでしょう。しかしそういうことも触れません。

Americans say that bombings of Japanese cities was necessary because there were many small factories located in Japanese neighborhoods. They do not say that the US Navy destroyed Japanese war industry by sinking 80% of Japanese merchant ships. With no raw materials to work with, the

第2章 日本陸海軍は本当に残虐だったのでしょうか？

factories shut down.

　アメリカ人は、日本の街には小さな工場がたくさんあったので、空襲する必要があったと言います。アメリカ海軍が日本の貨物船を約8割沈めていたので、日本の工場には製品を製造するのに必要な原材料がなく、工場はほとんど生産できない状態だった、という事実には触れません。

The bombings of Japanese cities was nothing but genocide. And it was deliberately planned.The American government built models of Japanese buildings in the American desert, and tested incendiary bombs on them.

　アメリカが行った日本の都市への空襲は、日本人大虐殺に他なりません。それはアメリカ政府が、入念に計画、準備して行ったものでした。アメリカは西部の砂漠に、大部分が木と紙でできた日本家

Some of the skulls of the many victims of Hiroshima some years later.
広島への原爆投下から数年後に発掘された多くの犠牲者の遺骨。

Chapter2 Were the Japanese Imperial Army and Navy brutal?

屋を再現したセットを造り、そこに焼夷弾を投下して、その効果を
検証しました。

One of the bizarre bomb tests involved the bat bombs. Small incendiary
devices were to be attached to bats. The live bats would be then placed in
a bomb canister, and dropped on a Japanese city. The bats would then fly
and seek shelter in Japanese houses. When the timer went off, the bomb
would explode, setting the house on fire. Many fires would be started at
the same time across a wide area, causing chaos and burning the city.

奇想天外なものに、コウモリ爆弾というものがありました。小さ
い焼夷弾を生きているコウモリに付け、それを爆弾の容器に入れて、
日本の都市に投下するというものです。爆弾容器から外へ飛び出し
たコウモリは木造家屋の中に逃げ込みます。タイマーでセットされ
た時間に焼夷弾が爆発して、その家で火災が発生します。これを広
範囲に渡って大量に投下すれば、都市のあちこちで火災が発生し、
都市は大混乱に陥る、という計画です。

But the bats set the the testing base in America on fire, this plan was
abandoned. In any case, it was cruel to Japanese people, and very hard on
the bats.

しかし、コウモリが実験基地を燃やしてしまい、米軍はこの計画
を断念しました。とにかく、日本人にもコウモリにも残酷な計画で
した。

Americans approach war as a means to exterminate other people. Japan
approaches war as a contest between warriors.

アメリカ人の戦争は敵国民を絶滅させるための行為であり、日本
人の戦争は武士同士の戦いです。

Americans accuse others of doing what they do. Last year, I visited a
museum in Tokyo, concerning the Imperial Japanese military medical

60

第2章　日本陸海軍は本当に残虐だったのでしょうか？

service. There was one exhibit, a model of a hospital ship. It was clearly marked as a hospital ship, both day and night.

　アメリカ人は自分たちがやっている悪行を他国がやっていると訴えます。昨年、都内にある日本軍の医療機関関係の博物館を訪問しました。そこに、軍の病院船の模型が展示されてあり、昼でも夜でも病院船だとはっきりと分かるマークが付けられていました。

But despite this marking, which was according to international law, more than half of Japanese hospital ships were sunk by America.

　戦争中、この国際法で定められたマークを付けた日本の病院船は、その半分以上がアメリカの攻撃で沈められました。

And America still does this today. In the Middle East, there are many bombing attacks being conducted by drones. They will shoot a missile at some person, killing people in the area. The drone will fly away, and circle back in about 30 minutes. They then shoot the ambulances.

　そして現在も、アメリカは同様の行為を繰り返しています。中東で、アメリカは多数の無人機を使って攻撃しているのです。ある人物を狙ってミサイルを発射し、その周りにいる関係のない人々も巻き込んで殺しています。無人機は現場から飛び去り、30分ほどで帰ってきます。さらに無人機は、救急車を狙ってミサイルを撃ち込みます。

Americans say the ambulances are probably carrying weapons. When questioned by news reporters on why so many extra people are being killed in drone attacks on suspected terrorist leaders, president Obama replied that anyone in the area near a terrorist leader is also a terrorist.

　アメリカ人は、その救急車には武器が積まれている可能性があると言います。ある時、記者がオバマ大統領に、なぜこれほど多くの関係ない人々が、テロリストのリーダーと疑われて、無人機で殺さ

61

Chapter2 Were the Japanese Imperial Army and Navy brutal?

れているのか、と質問しました。オバマ大統領の回答は、テロリストのリーダーの近くにいる人物は全員テロリストである、というものでした。

The truth of the matter is that only 2% of the people killed in drone attacks have been actual guerrilla fighters. The rest are other people. Americans invent new words to describe what the government does.

問題は、無人機の攻撃で殺害された人々のうち、実際にゲリラ兵だった者はわずか2%に過ぎなかった、ということです。その他の人たちは一般人です。アメリカ人は、このような政府の行為を正当化するために新しい言葉を創ります。

A Reaper drone carrying Hellfire missiles in use in the Middle East.

中東に投入された無人航空機 MQ-9 リーパー。ヘルファイア空対地ミサイルを搭載している。

第 2 章　日本陸海軍は本当に残虐だったのでしょうか？

People killed in American attacks who were not targets are called "collateral damage". When waterboarding or other torture is used on suspects, it is called an "Enhanced Interrogation Technique". It seems that Americans feel if they change the language, it makes the action better.

　攻撃目標ではないのに、アメリカの攻撃で殺害された人々のことを「副次的被害」と呼びます。容疑者にかける水責めその他の拷問は、「強化された尋問技術」と呼びます。アメリカ人は言葉を変えてしまえば、それらの行為がそれほどひどいものには感じないようです。

No it does not.

　しかし、言い方を変えたところで、やっていることは変わりません。

The truth of the Nanking incident
南京事件の真相

When discussing Japan in the Pacific War, Americans always bring up Nanking and Manila as examples of Japanese atrocities. Well at Nanking, I am convinced that rape and killing did happen. But it was a battlefield situation, and this has always happened with all armies in history. There was frankly, nothing unusual in this. War is a terrible affair.

　大東亜戦争中の日本について議論をすると、アメリカ人はいつも南京とマニラを、日本の残虐行為の例として持ち出してきます。まあ南京では、レイプや一般人の殺人が一部にはあったでしょう。しかし、これは戦場で起きたことで、歴史の中ではどこの軍でもこういうことがありましたし、あからさまに言ってしまえば、異例なことではありません。戦争とはそれほど恐ろしいものです。

Chapter2 Were the Japanese Imperial Army and Navy brutal?

What is very unusual about Nanking is that the Japanese Imperial Army restored discipline after the battle. General Matsui Iwane increased the number of military policemen, and when Hankow was attacked, such an incident was not repeated.

しかし、南京の場合、極めて異例なのは、戦闘の後、日本陸軍は規律を回復する努力をしたことです。松井石根将軍は憲兵隊の数を増やし、漢口を攻撃した時には、そのような問題は起こりませんでした。

And the Chinese KMT forces themselves, always killed and raped and robbed Chinese people. The commanders would not pay them, but keep the pay for themselves. When the troops were restless, the commanders would send them to nearby villages to rob and rape.

中国国民党の部隊は、いつも同胞であるはずの中国人に対してレイプ、強盗、殺人を働いていました。部隊長は兵士に俸給を与えずに、自分のポケットに入れていたので、兵士の不満がたまってくると、強盗やレイプをさせるために兵士を近くの村に行かせました。

China is a very large country, and many KMT troops were fighting in areas far from their own districts. So they would see nothing wrong with such behavior.

中国はとても広い国ですから、ほとんどの国民党軍の兵士は自分の故郷から遠い所で戦っていたので、そのような行為に罪悪も感じなかったのでしょう。

This was America's great strategic mistake of the war. They felt that if they destroyed Japan, a grateful Chiang Kai Shek would become America's servant in Asia. Not at all, he barely controlled his own army, they were a collection of warlords with only nominal loyalty to him.

ここで、アメリカは戦略的に大きな間違いを犯しました。日本を

第 2 章　日本陸海軍は本当に残虐だったのでしょうか？

叩き潰せば、蒋介石は大いに感謝して、アジアにおけるアメリカの召使いとなると考えていたのです。しかしそんなことは起こり得ませんでした。国民党軍は蒋介石に対する忠誠心に欠けた、複数の軍閥の寄せ集めでした。

He could not provide a stable China, or defeat the Communists. The Communists during the war treated the average Chinese peasant with respect. This great American mistake ensured that a Communist China would result. America should have cooperated with Japan to create a stable China.

蒋介石には安定した中国を作ることはできず、共産党軍に勝つこともできませんでした。このアメリカの戦略的な間違いによって、中国の共産化が確実なものになりました。アメリカの正しい選択は、日本と協力をして、安定した中国を作ることでした。

It was after the war that the Communist party started the Cultural revolution, and brought great tragedy upon China.

戦後、共産党の文化大革命で中国に悲劇が起きたのはご承知の通りです。

But the Japanese military had a much better record than the US military. Americans tend to cover up such bad incidents. There has always been much rape wherever US troops go. In fact, one third of female US troops themselves today are raped.

しかし、日本軍の実績はアメリカ軍よりもはるかに良いものでした。アメリカ軍がひどい事件を起こした時は、ほとんどの場合その事実を隠します。アメリカ兵が行く所、どこでもレイプ事件が発生します。実は、現在のアメリカ軍の中でも、女性兵士の約三分の一がレイプ被害にあっています。

65

Chapter2 Were the Japanese Imperial Army and Navy brutal?

How America evaded responsibility for the slaughter of the battle of Manila
マニラ事件はアメリカの責任転嫁

The battle of Manila is an instance of where the Americans blame Japan for what they did. Americans have always said that Japanese troops went berserk in the city, raping and killing, and this is why so many civilians died.

　マニラの戦いは、アメリカ人が自分たちがやったことを日本のせいにした一例です。マニラ市内で多くの一般人が死んだのは、狂暴な日本兵があちこちでレイプや殺人を犯したからだと、アメリカ人は言い続けています。

No. The truth is that the American advance was very slow into the city. This was of course due to the fighting by Japanese troops, but also American caution. Wherever American troops encountered a Japanese defensive position, it was bombarded with massive artillery and air strikes.

　それは事実ではありません。アメリカ軍は日本軍を警戒しながら、マニラ市内を慎重に前進しました。そして日本軍の抵抗を受けると、その防御陣地のあたりを徹底的に砲爆撃しました。

This is what killed so many civilians, and while it is possible that Japanese troops did kill some people, they could not have killed 100,000 people.

　それによって多くの一般人が死亡しました。その間、日本軍による殺人が何件かあったかもしれませんが、日本軍が 10 万人も殺害することは不可能です。

Only 1,010 Americans died in the battle, clearly saving American rather than Filipino lives was a priority.

66

第2章　日本陸海軍は本当に残虐だったのでしょうか？

　この戦いで、戦死したアメリカ兵は 1,010 人です。明らかにフィリピン人の命より、アメリカ兵の命を守ることの方が優先されていました。

In fact, the American conquest of the Philippines was very bloody. In the war from 1899 to 1913, somewhere around 1,000,000 Filipinos were killed. Waterboarding torture of Filipinos was common. Incidents such as the Balangiga incident were common. This was a village where the American general was angered by Filipino resistance. When the American military first occupied the village, the villagers and US troops got along well. But after a time, the Americans began to take their food and sexually assault the women. The villagers made an attack killing many US soldiers. The US commander ordered that the village and surrounding area be

Manila after being pounded by US artillery. 100,000 Filipinos were killed primarily by US air and artillery strikes in the battle. General Yamashita of the Imperial Japanese Army was blamed for the deaths post war and executed.

米軍の砲爆撃で廃墟と化したマニラ市街。10万人もの市民が犠牲となった。マニラ軍事裁判では山下奉文大将が、このマニラ大虐殺等の責任を問われ、絞首刑となった。

Chapter2 Were the Japanese Imperial Army and Navy brutal?

destroyed. After the battle, he executed every male person in the town over the age of 10 as punishment.

　実際に、アメリカのフィリピン征服は非常に残虐でした。1899年から1913年までの戦争で、およそ100万人のフィリピン人が殺害されました。米軍はフィリピン人をよく水責めの拷問にかけていましたし、バランギガ村虐殺のようなことはよく起きていました。アメリカ軍が最初にこの村に入った時は、村民とアメリカ兵の関係は良かったのですが、次第にアメリカ兵が村民の食料を盗んだり、村の女性に性的暴行を加えたりという事件が増えてきたので、村民がアメリカ兵を何人か殺しました。この村のフィリピン人の抵抗に怒ったアメリカの司令官が、その村とその周辺を徹底的に攻撃する命令を出しました。さらに、戦闘の後、罰として村の10歳以上の男子を全員死刑にしたのです。

Filipino Children being executed by American troops. this is from the the New York Journal. The caption reads" Kill everyone over 10".

米国兵によるフィリピン人銃殺を描いた『ニューヨーク・ジャーナル』の風刺画。後ろに「10歳以上の者は皆殺し」と書かれている。

第２章　日本陸海軍は本当に残虐だったのでしょうか？

I was in Japan in the US Marines in 1974 to 1976. I remember in 1975 we lost three Marines in Olongapo Philippines, where there was a major US Naval base. A Major, a Sergeant and a Private were in a jeep driving around the base perimeter. In a remote area they were killed. The jeep and their bodies were left behind, but heir heads were never found.

私は米国海兵隊員として 1974 年から 1976 年まで日本に派遣されていました。1975 年に、フィリピンのオロンガポ市にあった巨大な米海軍基地で３人の海兵隊が殺される事件があったのを思い出します。少佐、軍曹、二等兵が基地の近くをジープで移動中に起きた事件で、基地から離れた場所で死体が発見されました。ジープと死体が残されていましたが、頭部は見つかりませんでした。

Most Filipinos do like the US today, but not all. My command said it was Communists. But is seems that some Filipinos are still angry.

現在では、ほとんどのフィリピン人がアメリカを好きですが、もちろん全員ではありません。私の上官は共産主義の人間がこの事件を起こしたと言いましたが、アメリカを恨んでいるフィリピン人がいるのは確かでしょう。

Do not be fooled by American propaganda
アメリカのプロパガンダに騙されるな

People in America sometimes wonder why Japan fought so hard in the Pacific war. They cannot understand why Japan did not surrender early on in the war. To the American mind, Americans are a kind and gracious people, so why were Japanese people afraid of Americans?

アメリカ人は、大東亜戦争でなぜ日本があれほどまでに死に物狂いで戦ったのか、不思議に思っていますし、日本はなぜもっと早く降伏しなかったのか理解できません。アメリカ人が持っている自分

69

Chapter2 Were the Japanese Imperial Army and Navy brutal?

のイメージは、アメリカ人は優しく、親切な国民、というものです。
日本人がアメリカ人を恐れていた理由を理解できません。

So Americans rationalize this by saying that Japan's leadership was evil forcing Japanese to fight. No. This is pure propaganda.

それでアメリカ人は、悪い日本の指導者が、日本人に戦うことを強制した、と都合良い解釈をしています。それは事実ではありません。完全なプロパガンダです。

The American bloody conquest of the Philippines had only happened some 45 years before the Pacific war. Such incidents like the Balangiga incident happened many times, I am sure that Japanese leaders and people were aware of them. And the bombing of Japanese cities was genocide. These two incidents made it difficult to trust Americans.

アメリカによるフィリピンの血まみれの征服劇が起きたのは大東亜戦争の約45年前でした。その征服で、バランギガ村の事件のようなことは何度も起きていました。日本の指導者や国民はそんな事実を知っていたでしょう。そして、日本の大都市への空襲はまさに大虐殺でした。そういうことがあったので、アメリカ人を信用することが困難になりました。

After the war, Americans did not massacre Japanese people, even though rape and crime by US troops has been a never ending problem. But since the end of the war, America has been trying to remake Japanese society into one like America's.

戦後、アメリカ人は日本国民を虐殺しませんでした。しかし、米兵によるレイプその他の犯罪はずっと続いています。もう一つの大きな問題は、戦後、アメリカ人は日本社会をアメリカ社会のように作り直そうとしてきたことです。

This is a grave mistake. American society simply does not suit Japan, at all. And American society is fracturing, just look at the 2016 Presidential election. It would be better if Americans could be friends with Japan as it is, instead of trying to change it.

これは重大な間違いです。アメリカの社会は全然日本の社会には合いません。それに、2016年の大統領選を見てください、アメリカ社会は崩壊に向かっている最中です。アメリカ人が日本を変え、改宗させるのではなく、そのままの日本と真の友人となる方がずっと有益なことです。

Many Japanese do not respect their military
自国の軍隊を尊敬できない日本人

In America, saying that a person supports the troops is like a religion. Although, very few Americans actually do join the military themselves. But respect for one's own county's military is natural.

アメリカでは、軍隊を応援することは信仰のように自然なことです。とはいえ、実際に軍に入隊するアメリカ人は非常に少ないです。しかし、自分の国の軍隊を尊敬するのは当然のことです。

In Japan, we have an unnatural situation. Many Japanese people have no respect for the present day military, the Self Defense Forces, or for the Imperial Japanese Navy and Army.

日本は、不自然な状態にあります。多くの日本人には現代の日本軍とも言うべき自衛隊、それに帝国陸海軍に対して敬意があるように思えません。

This is not correct. It is because of the extreme efforts and sacrifice of the Japanese military that Japan is not a colony of the United States.

Chapter2 Were the Japanese Imperial Army and Navy brutal?

こういう状態は正しくありません。日本がアメリカの植民地にならずにすんだのは、日本軍の血のにじむような努力と犠牲があったからです。

Yes, America does have strong influence and power in Japanese domestic affairs. But because of the resistance of the Imperial Army and Navy, they could not completely dominate Japan. This effort to dominate Japan was an ongoing effort since the arrival of Commodore Perry's squadron.

確かに、アメリカは日本に対して強い影響力があります。しかし帝国陸海軍の抵抗で、日本を完全に支配することができませんでした。アメリカの、日本を支配するという野望は、ペリー来航以来、ずっと続いています。

And while President Obama's historic Presidential visit to Hiroshima shows that most Americans have deep hatred towards Japan, many in the US military have learned the value of military cooperation with Japan for the future.

オバマ大統領の歴史的な広島訪問で、多くのアメリカ人が今でも日本に対して嫌悪感を持っていることが明らかになりました。それと同時に、アメリカ軍人の多くが今後の日本との軍事協力の重要性を学びました。

I do not think I can convince many Americans of the truth of Japanese military conduct in the Pacific War, but Japanese people should learn and understand that truth. And also, for the people of the rest of the world outside America.

一般的なアメリカ人に大東亜戦争で日本軍が何を考えどう行動したのか、その事実を納得させることは不可能でしょう。しかし、日本人はその事実を学んで理解しなければなりません。そして、アメリカ以外の世界の人たちにもその事実を伝えるべきです。

Chapter 3

The East Asia Co-Prosperity Sphere
大東亜共栄圏

Europe and America feared the East Asia Co-Prosperity Sphere
欧米にとって脅威だった大東亜共栄圏

Americans in particular condemn the East Asian Co-Prosperity Sphere. It scares them. It was both an economic and political organization designed to exclude the Western, White, Christian powers from economic and military domination of Asia.

アメリカ人は特に大東亜共栄圏を非難しています。彼らにとって、それは恐ろしい存在でした。白人キリスト教国家によるアジアの経済的、軍事的支配を断ち切る、新たな政治的、経済的共同体だからです。

These White Christian powers still do not properly understand what Japan did. So they demonize Japan. When describing Japan's efforts with the Co-Prosperity Sphere, they inevitably use adjectives like oppressive, brutal, or inhumane.

白人キリスト教国家は今も日本がしてきたことを理解しておらず、日本を悪魔化しています。彼らが日本の大東亜共栄圏について述べる時は、いつも「圧政的」「残虐な」「非人道的」などの形容詞を使います。

Well these things Western White Christian powers understand, because this is how they act. I will now describe how Japan behaved in a totally

Chapter3 The East Asia Co-Prosperity sphere

different way. One reason I can do this is by my own experience in Japan. And another is we have a documented account of Japan's most stunning success, the annexation of Korea.

　まあ、そういう形容を、白人キリスト教国家はよく理解しています。彼ら自身が実際に、そのように形容される行為をしてきたのですから。これから日本の行動は欧米列強とは全然違ったという事実について説明します。どうしてそれをお話しできるかというと、私は日本に長く住んでおり、自分自身の経験があるからです。それから、実に見事な成功事例である、日本の朝鮮併合時代のことを記録した文書があります。

And those documented accounts are by Westerners themselves.

その文書は、西洋人が書いたものです。

Chandra Bose speaks at conference of the East Asia Co-Prosperity Sphere in 1943.

1943年に東京で行われた大東亜会議。アジア各国の首脳が集まった。参加各国の国旗の前で、チャンドラ・ボースが演説している。

第3章　大東亜共栄圏

First of all, what is a colony? It is basically a parasitic relationship between nations. The colonizing country sucks dry the resources of the colonized country. The only infrastructure that the colonizing country creates are the bare minimum needed to extract resources.

まず、植民地とは何でしょうか？　一般に、ある国が別の国に寄生するような関係のことです。植民地化した国が植民地化された国の資源を全て吸い尽くします。そして、その資源を吸い取るために必要な最低限のインフラしか造りません。

Education, public health of the populace is of little concern, as they cost too much. This is the Capitalist system at it's purest, drawing wealth from many to a very few privileged people.

その植民地の先住民に対する教育や公衆衛生にはコストがかかるので、宗主国は関心を持ちません。これは、最も純粋な資本主義システムです。数多くの人たちの財産がごくわずかな特権階級の人たちに吸い取られます。

Westerners created propaganda about colonialism, calling it "The White man's burden". They sincerely believed they were doing good by going around the world, destroying the societies of people in various countries, and taking their resources and wealth.

西洋人は植民地での活動についてプロパガンダを行い、「白人の責務」と呼びました。世界中の様々な国を侵略して、その国の文化と社会を破壊し、その国の資源と財産を収奪しましたが、白人は心から良いことをしていると信じていました。

From the Meiji restoration, Japan sought to survive in such a harsh world. The first thing to do was to create a strong Army and Navy, so that no Western power could take over and rule Japan.

明治維新以後、日本はそんな残酷な世界で生き残るための努力を

Chapter3 The East Asia Co-Prosperity sphere

しました。その第一は、欧米列強に日本が支配されないように、強い陸軍と海軍を持つことでした。

When expansion became necessary, they annexed Korea and Taiwan, and created a new state in Manchuria.

勢力圏の拡大が必要となると、台湾と朝鮮を併合して、満洲に新しい国家を創りました。

If America had not provoked Japan into all out war with the West, and instead worked with Japan, and if Korea and Taiwan were still part of the

Western style colonialism. Putting collars on aborigines.
白人による植民統治で、首輪をはめられた先住民たち。

76

Japanese Empire, and an independent Manchuko still existed, I think it is safe to say that China would not today be Communist.

もしアメリカが、日本を欧米列強との戦争に追い込むようなことはせず、逆に日本と協力していたら、朝鮮と台湾は今も日本で、満洲国はまだ存在しており、おそらく現在の中国は共産主義国家ではなかったでしょう。

The true nature of the East Asia Co-Prosperity sphere
大東亜共栄圏の真実

Having lived in Japan for 42 years, I know that Japan is an inclusive society. There is very little of the outright prejudice that exists in Western countries. People are expected to behave and act according to socially accepted rules. If you do this, you are accepted as one of society.

日本に 42 年も住んでいると、日本は共生の社会であるということ分かります。欧米のように明白な差別はほとんどありません。社会の常識に従って行動することを人々は期待しています。常識的な行動をすれば、社会の一員として受け入れられます。

Nearly every Westerner who comes here does not understand this. They bring the baggage of "assumed Western superiority", which is really colonial thinking.They cannot compromise and do things the Japanese way, because of inbred ideas that they are naturally superior.

日本にやってくる西洋人は、ほとんどこれを理解できません。「西洋人優越が当然」という荷物を携えてやってきます。これは本当に植民地的な考え方です。どうして彼らが日本の社会のルールに従わないのかというと、彼らは生まれながらにして西洋人が日本人、アジア人より優れた存在であると思っているからです。

Chapter3 The East Asia Co-Prosperity sphere

So very few Westerners do well in Japan.

そんなわけで、日本で問題なくやれる西洋人は少ないです。

One thing, Western countries do, Japan did not do. That was to require military service of countries under Japanese influence. Burmese troops, some 11,000 who fought for Japan, some 57,000 Indonesians,and Thais who allied with Japan, were not required to serve outside their home countries.

一つ、植民地において西洋国家が行い、日本が行わなかったことがあります。それは、自国の外での軍務を要求することです。日本と同盟関係にあったタイ軍、11,000人のビルマ軍、57,000人のインドネシア兵は、本国の外で戦うことは要求されませんでした。

Koreans were not required to serve in the military until nearly the end of the war.

朝鮮人には戦争末期まで徴兵はありませんでした。

This contrasts with Great Britain and France, both of which made extensive use of colonial troops. Germany had allied countries such as Italy, Rumania, and Hungary send troops into Russia.

それとは対照的に、英国やフランスは、植民地で数多くの兵士を募りました。ドイツの場合、同盟国、たとえば、イタリアやルーマニア、ハンガリー軍もロシアの前線へ送りました。

Japan did not require the countries allied with Japan to fight outside their borders. The Indian National Army was used in an invasion of India.

日本は同盟国の軍に対して、他の地域での協力を要求しませんでした。インド国民軍はインド攻略のために一緒に戦いました。

But the East Asia Co-Prosperity sphere really did not exist long enough to prove that Japan was truly interested in equality. Instead, we can look for this proof in the relationship Imperial Japan had with Korea.

しかし、日本がアジアの国々から搾取したのではなく、平等な関係を作ろうと努力したことを証明するには、大東亜共栄圏は短命すぎました。しかしその証拠は、日本と当時の朝鮮の関係を見れば分かります。

Let us examine this relationship.

それではその関係を見ていきましょう。

The Imperial Japanese Army and the Indian National Army fight together.

日本軍と行動を共にするインド国民軍の兵士たち。

Chapter 4

Why can't the Japan/Korea problem be solved?
日韓関係はなぜ修復できないのでしょうか？

The cause of all the trouble is Korea
トラブルの原因は常に韓国

I think most people in the world today are aware of the deep acrimony between Japan and Korea. One thing, it is all from the Korean side. Japanese people do not harbor ill will towards Koreans, but exasperation. It is the Koreans that express so much hate. In these following chapters I will explain why this is so.

世界の多くの人々は、日本と韓国は根の深い、ギスギスした関係にあることを理解していると思います。一つ言えるのは、このトラブルは全部韓国側が起こしているということです。日本人は韓国人に対して増悪というほどの悪い感情は持っていませんが、苛立っています。韓国人は日本人に対して強い憎悪の念を抱いています。この章では、そんな日韓関係についてお話しします。

First of all, it is not unusual for neighboring nations to have problems. When the Roman Imperial border stopped at the Rhine river, it ensured centuries of rivalry between France and Germany. Both Hungary and Romania were German allies in WWII, and sent troops to fight alongside Germany in the war in Russia. Yet the German military command had to put Italian troops in between them, out of fear that they would fight each other.

第4章　日韓関係はなぜ修復できないのでしょうか？

　まず、隣り合う国家間で問題があることは、世界の歴史をみても珍しいことではありません。ローマ帝国の境界線がライン川で留まったことで、ドイツとフランスは何百年間もライバルとして戦うことになりました。ハンガリーとルーマニアは第二次世界大戦では、両国共にドイツと同盟を結びました。両国は、ドイツと共にロシアで戦うために軍を派遣しました。しかし、ドイツの司令部は前線で両軍の間にイタリア軍を置きました。ハンガリー軍とルーマニア軍が隣同士だと、戦いが始まってしまうからです。

Well what about America? Ask any Canadian or Mexican what they think of America, you will get an idea. But there are some unique aspects of the Japanese/Korean relationship, and frankly this is because of the unusual nature of the Korean people.

　アメリカの評判はどうでしょうか？　カナダ人やメキシコ人に聞くと、彼らがアメリカを嫌っていることが分かります。しかし、日韓問題では、独特な様相が見られます。この原因は、率直に言うと、韓国人の異常とも言える国民性にあります。

First some basic history of both nations.

　最初に、両国の基本的な歴史を説明します。

Korean history
韓国の歴史

The first known Korean state, Gojoseon, was said to have been founded in 2333 B.C. Various states existed on the Korean peninsula, until in the first century of the Christian era the three kingdoms were formed. They were Goguryeo, which basically corresponded to modern day North Korea, Silla, which was the eastern half of modern South Korea, and Baekje,

81

Chapter4 Why can't the Japan/Korea problem be solved?

which formed the western half of present South Korea.

　朝鮮半島の最初の国、古朝鮮は、紀元前 2333 年に建国されたと
されています。その後いろいろな国が興り、紀元一世紀頃に、三つ
の王国ができました。ほぼ今の北朝鮮に位置する高句麗、今の韓国
東部に位置する新羅、西部に位置する百済、の三国です。

In 1392, the Joseon dynasty established itself over a unified country
in the Korean peninsula, and it is from this period which we concern
ourselves.

　1392 年に李氏朝鮮の時代が始まりました、今の日韓問題につい
ては、ここからが重要です。

Japanese History
日本の歴史

The Imperial family of Japan goes back more than 2,600 years, and
this was the first beginnings of a Japanese state. Although there is strong
opinion that the Jomon era could truly be considered the foundation of
Japanese civilization. This era began about 14,000 B.C.

　日本の皇室の歴史は、約 2,600 年前にさかのぼります。日本国の
始まりです。しかし、実際に日本文明が始まったのは縄文時代か
らだとする有力な意見もあります。縄文時代が始まったのは紀元前
14,000 年からです。

Culture and art gradually became more sophisticated in the Asuka, Nara,
and Heian periods. After the Heian period, warrior clans gained power,
then a time of civil war, called the time of warring states, lasted until the
overwhelming victory of the Tokugawa clan.

第4章 日韓関係はなぜ修復できないのでしょうか？

飛鳥時代、奈良時代、平安時代と続き、日本の文化、芸術は次第に洗練されていきました。平安時代の後、源頼朝が武士の頂点に立ち、鎌倉に武家政権が誕生し、その後戦国時代と呼ばれる内戦の期間が、徳川家の大勝利で終わるまで続きました。

This was followed by the Edo era, a time again renewed for the flowering of art and culture. With the Arrival of Commodore Perry's flotilla in 1853, Japan was forced to end it's period of seclusion from the world.

その次の時代が江戸時代です。江戸時代になると、芸術や文化がさらに発展しました。そしてペリー提督が来航して、鎖国下にあった日本に開国を迫りました。

Revolutionaries formed the Meiji government, which then embarked upon an ambitious era of reform. A modern Army and a Navy were built, and Western efforts to dominate Japan were resisted.

政治的革命によって明治政府が誕生し、それから野心的な改革の時代が始まりました。近代的な陸海軍を創設し、欧米列強による日本支配に対抗しようとしました。

It was at this time that Japan annexed Korea after soundly defeating Russia in the war of 1904 to 1905. It is from here we will begin.

1904 年〜 1905 年の日露戦争で大勝利した後、当時の朝鮮を併合しました。

The Yi dynasty class system
李氏朝鮮の身分制度

It is in the Joseon era that Korean antipathy towards Japan began. Let us

83

Chapter4 Why can't the Japan/Korea problem be solved?

see why.

　コリアの人たちが日本を毛嫌いし始めたのは、李氏朝鮮の時代からです。その理由を説明しましょう。

Korea at that time was a very traditionalist Confucian state. It was divided into several social classes, but the top class was of the Yangban or nobles. This rank was achieved by passing an examination in classical Chinese Confucianist literature. But since the exams were rigorous, and required extensive study, only those who could spend years in study could pass. In this way, the ruling class became basically hereditary.

　その時代、李氏朝鮮は伝統的な儒教の国でした。人々はいくつかの階級に分かれていました。一番上はヤンバン（両班）、貴族の階

Korean aristocrats play chess.

将棋を指す両班。

第4章　日韓関係はなぜ修復できないのでしょうか？

級でした。この階級に上がるためには、科挙試験に合格する必要が
ありました。その試験はとても難しいので、長い時間をかけて勉強
する必要があり、それが可能な人だけが合格しました。そうして、
この支配階級は実質的に世襲となりました。

Below this class was the Chungin,doctors, technicians and so forth.

その下は中人で、医者、技術者などでした。

Then there were Sangin who were basically farmers.

次は常民で、基本的に農家でした。

And next was the Chonin, entertainers, butchers and shamans. Various
historians may rank these classes differently, but this is a basic idea of their
status.

その下は賤人で、芸能人、屠殺者、シャーマンでした。歴史家に
よって、この分類やランクは違うかも知れませんが、これは基本的
な見方です。

There was a Baekjeoung untouchable class, which included prostitutes,
and below them were the Nobi, or slave class. Some 40% to 50% of the
population of Yi dynasty Korea was this slave class. It was hereditary.
Again, estimates of the percentage of slaves in Korean society differ, but it
was quite large.

次が、白丁、売春等の人たち、一番下は、奴婢、奴隷でした。李
氏朝鮮の人口は、４割から５割が奴婢で、それはほぼ世襲でした。
この割合も、歴史家によって違いますが、その人数はとても多いも
のでした。

Yes there were slaves in Korea. In Japan, there was indentured labor,
but never was a human being in Japan completely owned by another.

Chapter4 Why can't the Japan/Korea problem be solved?

And slavery still exists in Korea today. Recently, the British newspaper The Independent did an article about salt farms on remote islands off the southwestern Korean coast. They make salt from sea water, and it is back breaking work. To get labor, they kidnap mentally disturbed or homeless people from Seoul and hold them as slaves.

そうです。李氏朝鮮には奴隷がいました。日本では、契約労働はありましたが、人間が別の人の所有物になる奴隷制度はありませんでした。韓国には現在も奴隷がいます。最近の英国の新聞インデペンデントに、韓国南西沖の島にある塩田についての記事がありました。厳しい労働環境です。その労働に従事させるために、ソウルから、知的障害者やホームレスを誘拐してきて、奴隷として働かせていました。

The local police are in on the deal. If a slave escapes, the police send him back to the owner. Once Japan ruled Korea, slavery was abolished.

その島の警察は賄賂を貰っているので、この問題について動きませんし、奴隷が脱走した場合、警察が捉えてその脱走者を所有者に返しました。かつて日本が朝鮮を併合した時、奴隷制は廃止されました。

Literacy and culture in Yi dynasty Korea
李氏朝鮮の文化と識字率

In Joseon Korea, it was a state of extreme submission to the higher ranked people. Education for the common people basically did not exist. Literacy among the general populace was extremely low. In 1910, at the time of annexation, it was estimated to be about 6% of the population. Even though King Sejong the Great invented the Korean Hangul alphabet in 1446, its use was not encouraged by the Yangban nobility. They looked

第４章　日韓関係はなぜ修復できないのでしょうか？

down upon it as low class, proffering to use Classical Chinese. So literacy was low. Life expectancy in Yi Dynasty Korea was 24 for men and 26 for women. That is the same as uncivilized primitive man living in caves. We can compare this to Edo era Japan, where people could expect to live to 50.

　李氏朝鮮は、自分より階級が上位の人には逆らうことができない、完全な階級社会でした。一般庶民の教育は基本的に存在しなかったので識字率はとても低く、1910 年に日本が併合した時、約６％しかありませんでした。1446 年に朝鮮王世宗がハングルを公布しましたが、両班階級からは反発されました。彼らは、ハングルは中国の漢字より劣った、低俗な文字だと考えていたので、普及せずに識字率は低いままでした。李氏朝鮮における平均寿命は、男性が 24 歳で、女性は 26 歳でした。これは、洞穴に住んでいた原始人と同じです。その時日本は江戸時代でしたが、当時の日本の平均寿命は約 50 歳でした。

Except for the literacy and life expectancy issues, in a broad sense, we can that life in Yi Dynasty Korea was very similar to life in North Korea today.

　識字率と平均寿命以外、李氏朝鮮の生活は、だいたい今の北朝鮮に近いことがよく分かります。

Compare this to Japan. When American Commodore Perry arrived in Japan in 1853 to force Japan to trade with America, literacy among the general population in America was 40%, in Japan 80%.

　1853 年に、アメリカのペリー提督が日本に来た時、アメリカ人の識字率は 40%、日本人の識字率は 80% でした。

It was not until the annexation by Japan that the use of Hangul spread throughout Korean society, and that education for the masses was

87

Chapter4 Why can't the Japan/Korea problem be solved?

developed.

　日本が朝鮮を併合すると、一般庶民の教育が始まり、朝鮮全域で
ハングルが広く使用されるようになりました。

Confucianism is a strictly hierarchical system, and this was reflected in
Korean society of the time. There was little entertainment for the common
people, or no great culture. There were folk dances and such to be sure, but
there was little in the way of inspirational art developed by commoners.
Innovation was strictly repressed.

　儒教は厳しい階層的なシステムで、当時の李氏朝鮮の社会に根付
いていました。一般庶民のための娯楽はほとんどなく、優れた文化
もありません。フォークダンスのようなものは確かにありましたが、
一般の人に感動を与えるような芸術はありませんでした。革新的な
ものは厳しく抑えられました。

I think the Yangban looked down upon such things as being possibly
revolutionary in nature. In fact, the Korean military was mainly a force
to keep internal order. When called upon to fight a foreign invader, they
usually did poorly.

　両班はそういう芸術や文化的なものを見下していたのでしょう。
それに、社会の変革を刺激する可能性があるものとも考えていたの
でしょう。実は、李氏朝鮮軍は、国内の秩序を維持するために存在
していました。そのため、外国から侵略された場合、ほとんど役に
立ちませんでした。

The Nobles who ruined the country
国を滅ぼした両班

Intrigue among the noble classes was also debilitating to the nation. For

第4章　日韓関係はなぜ修復できないのでしょうか？

example, in the Imjin war, the Korean armies did very poorly against the invading Japanese forces. But one General did have great military ability, and was praised by Japanese Baron Konishi Yukinaga. His name was Kim. What was his reward for such success against Japanese forces? He was executed by jealous officials.

　両班の策謀は国を衰退させました。たとえば、秀吉の朝鮮出兵の時、侵攻する日本軍に、李氏朝鮮軍はほとんど勝てませんでした。しかし李氏朝鮮に軍事的な才能がある将軍が一人いました。小西行長が彼を称賛しています。その将軍は、金将軍。しかし、日本軍との戦いで活躍した彼の報酬は何だったでしょうか？　その活躍に対し、嫉妬深い両班が与えたものは死刑でした。

Admiral Yi Sun Shin deserves a lot of credit for forcing Japanese forces to abandon the Korean invasion. His invention of the turtle ship, and iron clad warship, and novel naval tactics could be said to have saved the nation. Well, at the time, Japan did not have a formal Navy, the seaborne part of Toyotomi's invasion was left to pirate Barons to handle. Yet Yi Sun Shin's reward was demotion to common seaman, he barely escaped execution.

　豊臣秀吉による朝鮮出兵は、陸の戦で勝っていても、徐々に撤退せざるを得なくなりました。その理由は、李氏朝鮮水軍の李舜臣将軍による戦略にありました。彼は亀甲船、装甲を施した軍艦を開発しました。当時の日本には本格的な水軍はなく、朝鮮出兵では海賊大名に任せていました。李舜臣の戦略は日本の水軍より一枚上手で、彼が李氏朝鮮を救いました。しかし、李舜臣への報いは、将軍から兵卒への降格でした。かろうじて死刑は免れました。

And corruption was omnipresent, to the point that the Korean justice system functioned only for the highest bidder.

　李氏朝鮮における司法制度は、最もお金を払う者が有利になるというもので、腐敗がはびこっていました。

Chapter4 Why can't the Japan/Korea problem be solved?

As we shall see, this intrigue among officials was one of the reasons Japan annexed Korea outright, Japan could not trust whether Korea would lean towards Russia or Japan. Such constant intrigue produced a government that was basically incompetent.

このような両班の策謀が、日本による併合をもたらした大きな理由の一つです。李氏朝鮮は日本側につくのか、ロシア側につくのか、日本は信用できず不安でした。そのような両班の策謀が常にあったため、李氏朝鮮の政府は無能でした。

And such strict adherence to Confucianist philosophy produced a nation with no artistic innovation, all artistic expression was frozen into an unchanging steady state form.

Yeongeunmun This was the gate where the Korean King performed Kowtow, or obeisance to the Chinese ambassador. After Japan's victory in the Sino Japanese war, it was torn down, the site is now an independence park.

迎恩門。朝鮮の歴代の王はここで、中国皇帝の勅使を三跪九叩頭（さんききゅうこうとう）の礼で迎えた。日清戦争で日本が勝利し、朝鮮が清の冊封体制から離脱すると、迎恩門は取り壊され、独立門が建てられた。

第４章　日韓関係はなぜ修復できないのでしょうか？

　そして、儒教の教えに固執していたため、あらゆる芸術的表現が
革新されることなく、旧態依然としたままでした。

Even the Korean Kings themselves had to have Chinese approval.
Whenever a new King was crowned, the Chinese Emperor would send
an ambassador. The ambassador would arrive outside Seoul, and read
an official document from the Emperor of China approving of the new
Korean King. The Korean King would go on his knees and bow his face
into the dirt before the ambassador from China.

　李氏朝鮮は国王が即位する時、中国の皇帝からの承認が必要でし
た。新しい国王が戴冠する時には、中国の皇帝が勅使を送ります。
勅使はソウルの迎恩門で、新国王を承認する中国皇帝からの文書を
読みます。李氏朝鮮の国王は、中国の勅使の前に膝まずいて、頭を
地面に付けます。

Korea was a complete vassal of China both politically and socially.
Japan, while having commerce with China, made no such submission.
Thus, the Koreans looked down upon Japan as barbarians, and considered
themselves superior.

　李氏朝鮮は、社会的にも政治的にも、完全に中国の属国でした。
日本は中国と貿易していましたが、服従関係にはありませんでした。
それで、李氏朝鮮時代の朝鮮人は、自分たちは日本より上位の国で
あり、日本は野蛮人の国だと思っていました。

Contrasting Yi dynasty Korea to the vibrant Edo era of Japan
李氏朝鮮と対照的だった江戸文化

Japan on the other hand, flowered in the Edo era. To the Westerner,
it may seem to be a contradiction. It was a military government that did

Chapter4 Why can't the Japan/Korea problem be solved?

not wage war. It was ruled by the Tokugawa clan. To be sure, there were enemy clans, most notably the Shimazu and Mori clans.

逆に、江戸時代に日本の文化は栄えました。西洋人は、そんなはずはないと思うかもしれません。徳川幕府は、戦争を行わない軍事政権でした。確かに、敵対的な藩、たとえば、毛利藩や島津藩はいました。

But they were kept in check by various checks set up in the government created by the Tokugawa. There was of course political intrigue and corruption, but it did not interfere with the administration of the country.

しかし、徳川幕府は上手に政治力を使い、行動を起こさせないための様々な制度を作り、その敵対的な藩をコントロールしました。もちろん陰謀や腐敗はある程度ありましたが、国の運営を妨げるほどのものではありませんでした。

Edo, Osaka and other cities in Japan were clean cities. There was a well organized water supply system, with underground wooden channels, and a waste disposal system, which included human waste. This was different from Korea, where it was simply thrown in the street, creating a malodorous environment, making deadly diseases endemic.

江戸、大坂、その他の日本の街は、どこも綺麗でした。特に江戸には上下水道ができていて、街中に木製の配管がめぐらされていました。そして、ゴミや糞尿を処理するシステムもありました。これは、李氏朝鮮とは全然違います。当時の朝鮮では、ゴミも糞尿もそのまま通りに捨てられていました。悪臭を放つひどい環境で、危険な風土病が蔓延していました。

And in Japan, during this Edo period, literacy was about 80% of population, while in Korea only the upper class, a tiny minority of the population could read and write.

それから、日本では、江戸時代の識字率は人口の８割でしたが、李氏朝鮮では、文字を読める人は一番上の階級でも少数でした。

The Edo era saw an extreme explosion of artistic creativity. Noh was for the noble classes, but for the common people Kabuki evolved. Ukiyoe paintings entertained people, along with it's erotic form, Shunga. Sumo wrestling was renewed as a national sport.

江戸時代は、芸術の創造性が爆発的に発展しました。能楽は貴族・武士階級に好まれ、平民の間では歌舞伎が大人気となりました。浮世絵も性的表現の春画も、人々を楽しませる娯楽として発展し、大相撲も人気を博しました。

There were just no equivalent to these entertainments in Korea, and modern day Koreans are jealous of this.

李氏朝鮮には、このような庶民も楽しめる娯楽は全くありませんでした。現在の韓国人はこのことをとても嫉妬しています。

The true reasons for the annexation of Korea
朝鮮併合の真実

There were many factors which contributed to the annexation of Korea by Japan. Basically, we can sum it up as strong Japanese efforts to survive, and Korean incompetence.

日本の朝鮮併合にはいくつもの理由があります。日本は独立国として生き残ろうとする強い意志と努力があったのに対し、李氏朝鮮は全く無能でした。

What do I mean? Well the arrival of Western powers carving out colonial empires in Asia was like a massive earthquake. China was weak

Chapter4 Why can't the Japan/Korea problem be solved?

and could not resist. Korea choose to ignore things and maintain its isolation.

無能というのはどういう意味でしょうか？　アジアに到達した欧米列強によるアジア植民地化の波は、まるで大地震のような衝撃をもたらしました。しかし清は弱くて、対抗できませんでした。李氏朝鮮はこの事態を無視する道を選んだのです。

In Japan, a coalition led by the Mori and Shimazu fiefs made a revolution and modernized the country. Everywhere Japan looked predatory Western powers lurked.

日本では、毛利藩と島津藩を中心とした連合が明治維新を起こして、日本を近代国家へと導きました。日本を欧米列強が虎視眈々と狙っているように見えました。

Korea was roiled by internal disorder. But unlike Japan, there was no capable force like the Western Barons, Mori and Shimazu to oppose the government. The revolutionaries were basically peasant armies. Since the Korean peasantry was illiterate, and with no experience of leadership, they could not organize effectively.

李氏朝鮮の国内は混乱するばかりでした。李氏朝鮮には、日本の毛利藩や島津藩のような有能な組織がありませんでした。李氏朝鮮の革命軍は基本的に農民の軍でした。李氏朝鮮の農民は読み書きができず、統率する経験もなかったので、まともな組織を作ることができませんでした。

Also the government forces, suffering from neglect and corruption, could not put the rebellions down, and chaos roiled the country.

李氏朝鮮の政府軍は、政府の怠慢と腐敗により、反乱を鎮圧できず、国が大混乱になりました。

第4章　日韓関係はなぜ修復できないのでしょうか？

The first Sino-Japanese war
日清戦争

A war between China and Japan.

それでは日清戦争について見てみましょう。

In 1894 China sent troops into Korea at the request of the Korean King.

1894年、清国は李氏朝鮮の王からの要請により陸軍の部隊を朝鮮に派遣しました。

The result was a war in which Japan soundly beat China. Despite the Chinese Navy possessing modern warships built in European yards, incompetence in training and discipline doomed the Chinese effort.

日本と清の間で戦争になりましたが、結果は日本の圧勝でした。清国海軍はヨーロッパで造られた最新の軍艦を持っていましたが、訓練不足で統率がとれておらず、その性能を生かすことができませんでした。当然敗北しました。

As part of the peace treaty, Japan occupied the strategic Liaodong Peninsula. It was at this juncture that Russia, Germany and France stepped in. They put diplomatic pressure on Japan to give up the Liaodong Peninsula. They were very condescending, saying that this sort of thing was not how a civilized country conducted itself.

講和条約の一つの条件に、日本にとって戦略的に重要な遼東半島の割譲がありました。これに、ロシア、ドイツ、フランスの三ヵ国が介入し、日本に外交的圧力をかけ、遼東半島を清に返還するよう勧告しました。それらの白人国家は日本に対して、非常に見下したように、文明国はそのようなことをしないと言いました。

Chapter4 Why can't the Japan/Korea problem be solved?

It was then that Russia moved in and built a major naval base on the Liaodong Peninsula at Port Arthur.

その後すぐにロシアが遼東半島に入り、旅順に海軍基地を置きました。

This is a thing I keep experiencing with Westerners. They keep saying that Japan should have stayed within her own borders, they say the Sino/Japanese war was the beginning of Japanese aggression. This is particularly true of Americans.

Chinese warship Dingyuan. She was scuttled after being damaged by a Japanese torpedo and shelfire. Built in Germany, at the time she was considered the most powerful warship in the Far East.

清国海軍の戦艦定遠。日本海軍の水雷艇の夜襲で損傷を受け、鹵獲を避けるため自沈。同型艦の鎮遠とともにドイツに発注、建造された戦艦で、当時東洋一の堅艦と呼ばれた。

第４章　日韓関係はなぜ修復できないのでしょうか？

　西洋人と話をしていると、何度も耳にすることがあります。彼らは、日本は自分の島に留まっておくべきで、日清戦争は日本の侵略政策の始まりだったと言います。アメリカ人は特にそう言います。

But they ignore the fact that they themselves, America included, were taking Empire by force all throughout Asia and the world. So how could Japan be bad by simply trying to survive? These same Westerners say that Japan should have depended upon Western powers for food, fuel, and steel, essential things for a modern nation.

　しかし、アメリカ人を含め西洋人は、自分たちの国が、世界各地を武力で植民地にして、帝国を拡げていた事実を無視しています。日本が生存のためにしたことがどうして悪なのでしょうか？　彼らは、日本は食料、燃料、鉄など、近代的な国家建設に必要な資源等を、西洋諸国に頼ればよかった、と言います。

But are Western countries truly benevolent? The truth of history shows us differently. Japan faces the same problem with the TPP treaty today. It is simply another form of colonial control, this time by American corporations. This conversation is simply another form of Western hate against Japan. What they mean is, Japan is an inferior country. Japan should never be allowed status equal to Western countries. This feeling continues today.

　しかし、欧米列強はそんなに親切な国なのでしょうか？　歴史を見ると、全然違うことが分かります。現在、日本は TPP の条約で同じ問題に直面しています。この条約は、形を変えた植民地支配です。今回はアメリカ政府ではなく、アメリカの企業です。先の会話は、西洋人の日本に対する単なるヘイトです。彼らは、日本が西洋より劣った国であり、日本が西洋と対等な立場に立つことを絶対に許さない、と言っているのです。この感覚は今も変わりません。

97

Chapter4 Why can't the Japan/Korea problem be solved?

The end stage of the Yi dynasty
末期状態だった李氏朝鮮

After the Sino Japanese war, Japan tried to help Korea stand up as an independent country. It proved to be impossible. There were no trained technocrat type people in the country at all. In the Meiji period, Japan sent people to Europe and America to be trained in skills to manage modern technology in all fields.

日清戦争後、日本が李氏朝鮮を独立国として立ち上がるよう援助しましたが、それは不可能でした。李氏朝鮮には専門的な技術官僚が一人もいなかったのです。明治維新では、日本が近代国家へと発展するために、欧米から様々な分野の最新の技術を学ぶために人材を派遣しました。

In Korea, nothing of the sort was done. In fact, the Korean court played games of intrigue between Japan and Russia. The Korean King even fled to the Russian embassy for protection for one year during one the many revolts of this period.

李氏朝鮮は、そんな行動を全く行いませんでした。実際に、李氏朝鮮は日本とロシアの間でいつまでも策謀ゲームを行っていました。この期間、反乱が頻発し、李氏朝鮮の国王は自分の命を守るためにロシア領事館に1年間隠れました。

There were Korean activists who wanted to Westernize their country, and survive as a Korean nation. One of the most notable was Kim Ok Gyun. He formed an independence party of like minded Yangban, He also admired Japan for its successful Meiji revolution, and studied at Japan's Keio university under the sponsorship of Fukuzawa Yukichi.

当時朝鮮を近代化して、朝鮮の独立を守りたいと考える活動家が

98

第4章　日韓関係はなぜ修復できないのでしょうか？

いました。有名な人物に、金玉均がいます。彼は同じ志を持つ両班と共に独立党を作りました。彼は、日本の明治維新の成功を模範として朝鮮の近代化を目指し、福澤諭吉の支援を受け、慶応義塾で学びました。

Eventually, he made a successful coup in Seoul, but the plan had been betrayed to the Queen, who called to the Chinese Army for help. The coup members fled to Japan.

Kim Ok Gyun, Korean revolutionary and reformer. His revolution was betrayed, he was assassinated, his dismembered body displayed throughout Korea.

金玉均。李氏朝鮮後期の政治家で朝鮮独立党の指導者。明治維新を模範として清からの独立と朝鮮近代化を目指したが、クーデターに失敗して日本に亡命。その後上海で暗殺され、バラバラにされた遺体は朝鮮各地で晒された。

Chapter4 Why can't the Japan/Korea problem be solved?

　彼はソウルでクーデターを起こしましたが、皇后が清軍に助けを求めたため、結局はクーデターを実行したメンバーは日本へ逃れました。

In 1893, while on route to Shanghai from Japan to visit another revolutionary, Kim Ok Gyun was assassinated. His body was sent to Korea, where it was dismembered, and the various body parts put on public display in various towns throughout the nation.

　1893 年、他の革命家と会うために、日本から上海に渡った時に暗殺されました。彼の死体は朝鮮へ送られ、そこでバラバラに切断され、死体の各部がいくつかの街で晒されました。

The Russo-Japanese war
日露戦争

The Russian Japanese war resulted because of continued encroachments by Russia into Korea. Russian companies operated in Korea. But they secretly were constructing Naval bases. One was to be located at Masan, near the present city of Pusan.

　日露戦争の原因は、ロシアによる朝鮮への侵略です。ロシアの会社が朝鮮内で活動していました。しかし、実は密かにロシアの海軍基地を造っていました。その海軍基地の計画の一つは馬山で、現在の釜山市の近く、対馬の目と鼻の先でした。

This was intolerable to Japan, and the Russo/Japanese war resulted, which was an overwhelming victory for Japan.

　日本はそんなことを許容できず、日露戦争が起こりました。

While the Russian soldiers and sailors fought much more bravely than

100

第4章 日韓関係はなぜ修復できないのでしょうか？

Chinese or Korean troops, their leadership was incompetent. Their only decent military leader was admiral Makarov, who energetically led the Russian fleet at Port Arthur.

　清軍や朝鮮軍より、ロシアの兵士はとても勇敢に戦いましたが、ロシアの指揮官はほとんど役に立ちませんでした。唯一まともなロシアの指揮官は、海軍のマカロフ提督で、旅順港のロシア艦隊を強力に統率しました。

Admiral Stepan Makarov, one of the Great officers of the Imperial Russian Navy. He was first in the world to launch a torpedo attack, against the Turkish fleet, and he developed the basic concept of torpedo warfare.

ロシア帝国海軍中将ステファン・マカロフ。海軍戦術論の大家で、オスマン帝国の警備船に対して世界初の雷撃を敢行、自身の水雷艇戦術理論を実践した。

Chapter4 Why can't the Japan/Korea problem be solved?

He had 7 battleships there to Japan's 6, he could have made things very difficult for Japan. But his flagship struck a mine on returning to Port Arthur, and sank within minutes. The next commander of the Pacific fleet remained in Port Arthur, declining to engage the Japanese fleet in combat.

日本の戦艦6隻に対し、旅順港のロシア艦隊は戦艦7隻でした。マカロフ提督は、日本にとって非常にやっかいな存在でした。しかし、彼が座乗する旗艦は、日本艦隊との海戦の後、旅順に帰投する時に日本軍の敷設した機雷に接触し、数分で沈没しました。次のロシア太平洋艦隊の司令官は、旅順港にこもって、日本艦隊との海戦を避けていました。

Japan won the war overwhelmingly.

日本は日露戦争で大勝利をおさめました。

Chapter 5

The truth of the annexation period
併合時代の真実

Examining documents of the annexation period
併合当時の資料を読む

So Japan decided that outright annexation and rule by Japan was the only possible solution. Again, many Westerners insist that it was a brutal occupation. But was it? Very fortunately, we have some observations by a professional observer, Mr. Alleyne Ireland. He was British. He was appointed by the University of Chicago as a Colonial Commissioner, and sent to the Far East to study the American, Japanese, Dutch, British and French Colonial systems.

それで、日本は朝鮮を併合するしか解決策はないと判断しました。これについても西洋人から、残酷な占拠政策だったという声がたくさん聞かれます。しかし、それは本当でしょうか？ 幸いなことに、有力な目撃者の証言があります。その人物は、アレン・アイルランド。英国人です。アメリカのシカゴ大学から植民地運営研究の委員に任命され、アメリカ、日本、英国、オランダ、フランスの植民地統治システムを調査するために極東に派遣されました。

The following statistics that I use are all from his book "The New Korea". He visited Korea in 1922, and published his book in 1926.

以下の統計は、全て彼の著書『The New Korea』からの引用です。彼は 1922 年に日本併合時代の朝鮮を訪問し、1926 年にその著作

Chapter5 The truth of the annexation period

を出版しました。

I truly think that to describe the Japanese annexation of Korea, we should use the word "uplift".

私は、日本の朝鮮併合について語るには、「向上」という言葉を使うべきだと思います。

Let us begin with Mr. Ireland's account of Korean society in 1922.

アイルランド氏による、1922年当時の朝鮮社会についての報告から始めましょう。

After the Sino/Japanese war, Japanese officials were appointed by the Korean King to administer the country. This idea was put forth by Japan. The problem was, the Korean government had not sent any Koreans to be trained in the West in modern techniques of government.

日清戦争後、李氏朝鮮の国王は国家運営のために日本人顧問を任命しました。この提案は日本側から出されたものですが、問題は李氏朝鮮の王室は朝鮮人を西洋へ派遣していなかったので、近代的な国家運営法を理解している朝鮮人がいなかったことです。

After the annexation, even though Japan ruled Korea directly, every effort was made that Koreans would be trained in modern government, and promoted through the ranks.

併合後、日本が朝鮮を直接統治しましたが、近代的な政府の中で朝鮮人に体験を積ませ、その技能向上のためのあらゆる努力がなされました。

Local government was completely built up from scratch.

地方政府はゼロから構築されました。

104

第5章　併合時代の真実

On the provincial level, for budget purposes, five departments were created; Public Works, Sanitation and Hospitals, Relief and Charity, Industrial encouragement, and Education.

地方政府は予算を組み、公共事業、医療・衛生、社会・慈善、産業奨励、教育の5つの部門を作りました。

A view of Seoul before and after annexation.
日本統治前と後のソウル。

105

Chapter5 The truth of the annexation period

No such organization had existed in the Yi dynasty Korea. These organizations promoted the welfare of the Korean people. For example, the Koreans often say that the mountains are bare of trees because Japan cut down all the trees. The opposite is true. The forests were destroyed by corrupt Yi dynasty officials. Under the above Industrial encouragement, forestry seedling stations were established at the local level throughout Korea.

李氏朝鮮の時代にはこのような組織は存在しなかったので、これにより朝鮮人の福祉が向上しました。たとえば、今の韓国人は韓国の山に木がないのは、日本人が併合時代に全ての木を伐採したためだ、とよく言いますが、事実は逆です。腐敗した李氏朝鮮の両班によって朝鮮半島の山林崩壊が進んでいましたが、上記の産業奨励により、植林のための事業所が朝鮮半島全域に造られたのです。

In the field of Law
法律

In YI dynasty Korea, law was administered by court appointed officials. They were all corrupt, and verdicts were handed out to highest bidder. Torture was commonly used, both on suspects and witnesses. This was to gain the desired verdict.

李氏朝鮮では、王室から任命された両班が法を管理していました。その全てが腐敗しており、判決は最も多額の賄賂を渡す人物に有利になりました。賄賂を渡さない容疑者も目撃者も拷問されました。それは自分たちが出したい判決に有利な証言をさせるためです。

After annexation, in general, Japanese law became the law of the land. An exception was made for the crime of murder. Korean penalties were kept in this case. This was because the punishments mandated by Japanese

第 5 章　併合時代の真実

law were considered too mild to have an effect upon Korean crime. At this
time, murder was quite common in Korea.

　併合後は、基本的に日本の法律を使いました。しかし殺人の場合
は例外で、李氏朝鮮の法律がそのまま適用されました。当時の朝鮮
では殺人事件がよく起きていたのですが、日本の法律は殺人罪の刑
罰が軽く、犯罪の抑止効果が弱かったからです。

Flogging was refined so that women and children and the mentally
disabled could not be punished by it. It was banned altogether in 1920.

　むち打ち刑は、女性、子供、知的障害者には行わないように法律
が改正され、1920 年にはむち打ち刑は廃止されました。

In Yi dynasty Korea there was no set court system. Often corrupt local
police stations conducted trials and punishments on their own.

　李氏朝鮮では、まともな裁判制度はなかったので、よく地方の警
察署が勝手に裁判と刑罰を実行していました。

Under Japanese rule this was abolished, by 1909, there was one supreme
court, 3 courts of appeal, 8 local courts 9 branch local courts and 80
district courts.

　日本統治ではこれは廃止され、1909 年までに、朝鮮に高等法院
1 ヵ所、覆審法院 3 ヵ所、地方法院 8 ヵ所、地方法院支庁 9 ヵ所、
地方法院出張所 80 ヵ所が造られました。

In 1923 there were 162 Japanese and 37 Korean judges, 67 Japanese and
10 Korean public prosecutors, and 432 Japanese and 232 Korean clerks
and assistant interpreters.

　1923 年には、日本人 162 人、朝鮮人 37 人の判事、日本人 67 人、
朝鮮人 10 人の検察官、日本人 432 人、朝鮮人 232 人の書記官と補
助通訳官がいました。

107

Chapter5 The truth of the annexation period

When one considers that before Japanese involvement in the internal affairs of Korea before the Sino/Japanese war of 1894 the number of Koreans who had an education qualifying themselves in modern legal affairs was zero, this is quite an accomplishment in 29 years.

1894年の日清戦争以前、日本が李氏朝鮮の内政に関わる前は、法律の分野で、最新の専門教育を受けた朝鮮人の数がゼロだったことを考えると、29年間でこの数字は日本の偉業といえます。

The number of courts by 1925 had expanded to 1 Supreme Court, 3 Courts of Appeal, 11 local courts, 46 branches of local courts, 160 detached or local courts.

1925年までに法廷の数は、高等法院1ヵ所、覆審法院3ヵ所、地方法院11ヵ所、地方法院支庁46ヵ所、地方法院出張所160ヵ所にまで拡大しました。

And corruption, bribery was non existent.

腐敗、賄賂は完全になくなりました。

The police system
警察制度

In Yi dynasty Korea, police functions were carried out by military garrisons throughout the country. There was no independent professional police force. In general this force abused the local population, and acted in the interest of rich and powerful people.

李氏朝鮮において、警察の業務は地方に駐屯している軍守備隊が行い、独立した組織としての警察はありませんでした。基本的にこの警察業務を行う軍守備隊は、地元住民を虐待し、金持ちや権力者

第 5 章　併合時代の真実

の利益のために行動しました。

In 1894 Japan created a police force separate from the military, and established a school in Seoul to train police officials. This did not prove sufficient to create a professional force however.

　1894 年に日本が軍隊とは別に、独立した組織として警察を創り、ソウルに警察官を養成する学校を造りました。しかし、これだけでは、まともな警察組織を作るにはまだまだ十分ではありませんでした。

So in 1904, a large number of Japanese police were brought in to introduce professionalism in the ranks. In 1909, there were 36 Japanese and 11 Korean inspectors, 156 Japanese and 102 Korean sergeants, 1,924 and 57 Korean interpreters, 63 Japanese physicians.

　そのため、1904 年に多数の日本人警察官が、当時の朝鮮人に専門的な業務を教えるために、日本から送り込まれてきました。1909 年には、日本人 36 人、朝鮮人 11 人の警部、日本人 156 人、朝鮮人 102 人の巡査部長、日本人 1,924 人、朝鮮人 57 人の通訳官、日本人医師 63 人がいました。

There are many museums in Korea, with plaster mannequins showing the torture of Korean people by Japanese soldiers. One, Japanese soldiers basically did not interfere in day to day affairs in Korea. Two, throughout the annexation, most rank and file police in Korea were ethnic Koreans.

　今の韓国には、日本兵が朝鮮の一般市民を拷問する様子を、蝋人形を使って展示している博物館がたくさんあります。これに対する反論は、一つ、日本陸軍は、当時、基本的に朝鮮の内政に関わっていなかったこと、二つ、併合時代、警察官の多くは朝鮮人だったこと、です。

If such torture did indeed exist, Mr. Ireland would have certainly

109

Chapter5 The truth of the annexation period

mentioned it, as he was a neutral observer. Instead he notes that Yi dynasty Korean punishments were much harsher than Japanese.

もしそんな拷問が本当にあったのなら、アイルランド氏は中立の立場でしたので、間違いなくそのことを本に書いていたでしょう。彼が書いているのは、日本併合時代より李氏朝鮮時代の罰の方がはるかに厳しい、ということです。

And this is part of the reason for Korea screaming about Japan today. They know themselves in their hearts, but they truly don't understand Japan. So they ascribe the more terrible characteristics of the Korean soul to Japan.

そしてこれが、今も韓国人が日本に罵声を浴びせる理由のひとつです。自分たちのことはよく理解していても、日本人のことは全く理解していません。コリアンはひどい性質なので、日本人も自分たちと同様にひどい性質であると考えます。

Between the Sino/Japanese war and the annexation, a gendarme force was created to deal with bandits. All throughout Korean history, there had been marauding gangs of bandits throughout the country. By 1909, there were 2,369 Japanese and 4,392 Koreans stationed at 499 posts in the gendarme in the peninsula.

日清戦争と朝鮮併合の間、日本は盗賊を取り締まるために憲兵隊を創りました。朝鮮はその歴史を通して、盗賊が半島全域にいました。1909年までに、日本人2,369人と朝鮮人4,392人の憲兵が朝鮮半島の499ヵ所に配置されました。

In 1922, the number of police was 1,161 Japanese and 422 Korean officers, and 11,028 Japanese and 8,160 policemen in Korea. The total population was 17 million.

1922年には日本人1,161人、朝鮮人422人の警察官僚、日本人

110

11,028 人、朝鮮人 8,160 人の警察官がいました。当時の朝鮮の人口は 1,700 万人でした。

Conditions in Yi dynasty prisons were terrible. They were very overcrowded. When Japan took over, it was found that the average prisoner had only 5 square feet of space. Japan reformed the system totally, and Mr. Ireland states that Japanese run prisons in Korea were better than most American prisons of the day.

李氏朝鮮の監獄は、囚人に対して恐ろしくひどい扱いで、非常に過密した状態にありました。日本が引き継いだ時に、囚人一人当たりの面積は 0.5 平方メートルしかありませんでした。日本は朝鮮の監獄の体制を全面的に改めました。その結果、アイルランド氏は、日本統治下の朝鮮にある刑務所は当時のアメリカにあるたいていの刑務所より良い状態だったと書いています。

Death rates of prisoners was low. In the five years ending in 1923, the average daily prison population was 15,220, and the average annual death rate was 288. The tales that Korean people tell of torture and murder by Japanese police in Korean prisons are simply myth.

囚人の死亡率は非常に低く、1923 年までの 5 年間の、囚人の平均数は 15,220 人で、年平均の死者は 288 人です。今の韓国人が言う、日本の警察官が当時の朝鮮人を拷問して殺したという話は、全くの神話です。

Finance
財務

In Yi dynasty Korea, finances were chaotic to say the least. There were two financial departments of the Yi dynasty government, that of the State

Chapter5 The truth of the annexation period

and that of the Royal household. They were supposed to be independent of each other, but the Royal household often took funds from the State financial department.

李氏朝鮮の財政は無秩序状態にありました。李氏朝鮮では二つの財務部門がありました。王室と国の財務です。お互い独立した形でしたが、王室の財務から、国の財務部門が勝手に資金調達をすることが度々ありました。

There was much abuse and thievery that went with the collection of taxes. Rights to mint coinage, that competed with the national currency were sold to the highest bidder. So it can be said that Yi dynasty Korea did not possess a trustworthy currency.

税金の徴収にあたっては、たくさんの不正、乱用がありました。硬貨を鋳造する権利は、最も高い賄賂を払った者に与えられていたため、李氏朝鮮では信用できる通貨がありませんでした。

As Japan took over administration of the country, land registration was clarified so as to provide a reliable tax base, a central bank was established along with a reliable currency, this was all subsidized by loans from Japan.

日本の朝鮮統治後、土地の所有者を登録したことで、どこからどのように税金を取ればいいかが明確になりました。税金を徴収する基準がはっきりし、中央銀行が信用できる通貨を流通させました。こういった活動は全て日本からの融資によって助成されたのです。

Education
教育

The first formal Korean education system was begun in 1398 when the the founder of the Yi dynasty, King Tai-cho, (Ri Song Ge) established a

第5章　併合時代の真実

university in Seoul. Schools were also established in the provinces.

　昔の朝鮮における教育制度は、1398 年に始まりました。李氏朝鮮の太祖、李成桂が漢城（ソウル）に大学を設立し、地方にもそれぞれ学校を設立しました。

The third Yi dynasty king, Tai-chong added preparatory schools. These were supported by government farms that were worked by slaves. Instruction was given in Chinese literature, so that students could pass the examination for officials.

　三代国王、太宗は予備校を創りました。この予備校は奴隷が働く農家の収益から経費が出されていました。教育内容は中国の儒教に基づいており、それは両班になるための試験に合格するのに必要な知識でした。

There were also privately run schools called Seodang which taught written Chinese.

　書堂という、中国語の読み書きを教える私塾もありました。

As long as Korea lived in isolation, this system which could only produce a Confucian scholar, was good enough. But when Western powers began to encroach upon Asia, such scholars could not comprehend what was happening.

　鎖国下にある李氏朝鮮においては、儒学者を作るだけに過ぎないこのシステムで十分であると考えられていました。しかし、西洋諸国によるアジア侵略が始まっても、この儒学者たちは、その先行きを全く理解できませんでした。

As Japan took over administration of the country, change was rapid. At first three things were done. One was to establish schools for girls. The Korean government had not done anything in this area.

113

Chapter5 The truth of the annexation period

　日本は、併合後まず三つのことを行い、朝鮮に急速な変化をもたらしました。一つ目は、女性のための学校設立です。李氏朝鮮政府は、女性の教育に対して何も対応をしていませんでした。

The second was the establishment of Commercial, Technical, and Agricultural schools. Baron Okura of Japan personally funded a private Commercial school in 1906.

　二つ目は、商業、工業、農業の学校設立です。1906 年、日本の大倉男爵は私立の商業学校設立に莫大な資金を提供しました。

The third thing done was to place private schools under the supervision of the government. Before this time, there had been no attempt to control them. Standards of education varied widely, many were schools in name only, which existed simply to make money.

　三つ目は、公立学校を設置することです。日本統治以前の朝鮮には、公立学校はありませんでした。教育の程度はいろいろありましたが、多くは金儲けのための名ばかりの学校で、教育のレベルはひどいものでした。

Standards were set and approved textbooks distributed.

　教育の水準が決められ、政府が承認した教科書が配布されました。

As Japanese people came to settle in Korea, a dual system was set up. At first, Korean and Japanese children went to separate schools. This could not be helped, as the gap was too wide in education. As time went on, schools for children who spoke mainly Korean, and for those who spoke mainly Japanese were created. Children of either Korean or Japanese ethnic background could attend the school of their choice.

　日本人が朝鮮半島に住むようになると、二つの平行したシステムが作られました。最初は日本人と朝鮮人の子供が別の学校へ行きま

第5章　併合時代の真実

した。これは、教育水準に差がありすぎたので仕方がないことでした。徐々に、普段朝鮮語を使う子供と日本語を使う子供が同じ教室で学ぶ学校が増えていきました。日本人、朝鮮人の子供は通いたい学校を選ぶことができました。

The fact is, many of the Japanese who settled in Korea learned to speak Korean.

実際は、当時朝鮮半島に住んだ日本人の多くが、朝鮮語を話せるよう朝鮮語を学びました。

A Korean textbook in use during the annexation period. Notice it teaches the Korean Hangul script.

日本統治時代に学校教育で使用された朝鮮語読本。

Chapter5 The truth of the annexation period

As far as Christianity is concerned, there was no discrimination. Schools that wished to have government verification, could not teach the Bible during school hours. But there was no prohibition of Bible study after regular school hours.

キリスト教に対する差別はなかったので、政府認可の学校においては、正規の授業で聖書を教えることはできないものの、それ以外の時間であれば問題ありませんでした。

There were sometimes Shinto religious ceremonies with students. Shinto was the State religion of Japan, and Korea had been annexed after all. However, Christian students could be excused from such ceremonies due to their beliefs.

神道の儀式に生徒が参加する機会がありました。神道は当時の日本の国教でしたが、キリスト教の学生が、自分の信仰とは違うという理由で、その儀式に参加しなくても問題ありませんでした。

Medical services
医療

In the Yi dynasty, medical services were performed by exorcists and shamans practicing folk medicine. No trained doctors existed in the country.

李氏朝鮮では祈祷師や呪術師が民間医療を行っており、医学を専門的に学んだ医者は存在しませんでした。

On the advice of Japan, the Korean government in 1897 issued instructions for vaccination against cholera, typhoid, diphtheria, and dysentery. However, the Korean government was unable to carry them out.

116

第 5 章　併合時代の真実

1897 年に、日本は、当時の朝鮮政府に、赤痢、ジフテリア、腸チフス、コレラの予防接種を行うよう助言しました。しかし、専門的な医者がいなかった当時の朝鮮政府には、それを実行することは不可能でした。

Before the Japanese annexation, Korea did have a medical school, and a few Christian medical schools, but the equipment of these was very poor. So once annexation happened in 1910, The Japanese government built hospitals and made efforts to eradicate disease throughout the country.

朝鮮併合前に、医療学校が 1 校といくつかのキリスト教系医療学校がありましたが、それらの学校の設備はとても質の悪いものでした。1910 年の併合後、日本政府は病院を建設し、半島全域で病気を撲滅するよう努力しました。

As we have seen, there was no type of waste disposal, even in Seoul, so a mammoth effort had to be made to reach people modern sanitary habits. The Japanese government also established facilities for producing clean drinking water.

漢城（ソウル）でさえゴミや人糞を処理する習慣は全くなかったので、当時の朝鮮人に近代的で衛生的な習慣を根付かせるのに多大な努力が必要でした。清浄な水を作る施設が設置されたのも日本が統治してからです。

In this regard, a Central Health Agency, Hygienic Inspection Agency for inspecting the purity of food, beverages and drugs, a Bacteriological service for control of infectious diseases, and an Opium control office, to fight opium addiction, were all established.

その後、食料、飲料、薬品の衛生検査を行う中央衛生会が設置され、感染症を検査する細菌研究所や、アヘン中毒をなくすための施設も設置されました。

Chapter5 The truth of the annexation period

Government qualification standards were also established for doctors.

政府が定めた医師の資格も作られました。

At the time of the annexation, the Imperial Japanese government also established a fund for disaster relief for Korean people. For example, a major drought occurred in 1919. Due to this fund, no one starved to death in Korea.

併合の時に、日本帝国政府は朝鮮人のために災害救済基金を作りました。たとえば、1919年に朝鮮で大干ばつがありましたが、この救済基金があったおかげで、その干ばつが原因で餓死した人は一人もいませんでした。

Agriculture
農業

During the Yi Dynasty, land ownership was unclear, and agricultural techniques chaotic. In land ownership disputes, magistrates always ruled in favor of the richest party. The plight of the Korean farmers, 80% of the population, was poor.

李氏朝鮮においては、土地の所有権は不明確で、農業技術も低劣なものでした。所有権の問題では、裁判官は常に金持ちの方に有利な判決を下しました。人口の8割を占める李氏朝鮮の農家の状況はひどいものでした。

Japan established modern agricultural schools, credit banks, allowing farmers to purchase the land they worked by time payments, and improved agricultural implements.

日本は近代的な農業学校や朝鮮殖産銀行を設立しました。この銀

第5章 併合時代の真実

行を利用することで、農民が割賦で自分の農地を購入することが可能になり、農器具を改善することもできました。

The average Korean had difficulty in understanding the credit system, as they could only comprehend it as another form of governmental thievery. Well, that was all they had known throughout their history. It took much time to understand the concepts of modern finance, banking, and reliable currency.

The Chosen Industrial bank main office. There were over 50 branches, providing non collateralized loans to light industry and farmers.

朝鮮殖産銀行本店。50余の支店を有し、農工業者への無担保貸付を行った。

Chapter5 The truth of the annexation period

当時の一般的な朝鮮人は貸付制度を理解できなかったので、政府が国民からお金をだまし盗る方法なのだと思っていました。まあ、彼らの歴史では常にそのようなことが繰り返されていたので無理もありません。近代的な金融、銀行、信用できる通貨の概念を理解するまで、長い時間がかかりました。

To show the increase in agricultural production after annexation, we have the following figures. It is given in thousands of koku, 1 koku equals 5 bushels.

日本併合後の農業生産力の増加を示すものとして、下記の数字があります。単位は 1,000 石です。1 石は 5 ブッシェルです。

	米（Rice）	大麦（Barley）	豆（Beans）
1912	10,865	5,856	4,733
1923	15,175	6,031	5,855

The improvement in agriculture is clear, which led to an increase in the population.

農業生産力の増加は明らかです。そのため、人口が増えました。

The fishing industry did not exist except in some very local areas under the Yi dynasty. Fishing was developed into an industry under Japanese rule.

いくつかの地方を除いて、李氏朝鮮では漁業は産業として存在していませんでした。日本の統治によって、漁業が半島全域で発展しました。

第 5 章　併合時代の真実

Japan builds Korea's entire modern infrastructure
日本が朝鮮のインフラを整えた

Japan completely built Korea into an industrialized state. Factories and dams were built throughout the country. The showpiece was the city of Hungnam in what is now North Korea.

日本は当時の朝鮮を近代的な産業国に造り変えました。全国に工場やダムが建設されました。特に著しく発展した都市は現在の北朝鮮の興南区域でした。

From a simple fishing village, under Japanese rule, it was built into a completely new industrial city with a population of hundreds of thousands in a few short years.

日本統治により、数年間で小さな漁村から数十万人の人口を擁する大都市に発展したのです。

The Chosin reservoir dam, built by Japan to supply the complex with electricity, was the site of one of the US Marine Corps most famous battles in the Korean war.

その大都市に、電力を供給するために日本が造った長津湖ダムは、朝鮮戦争で米海兵隊が戦った激戦地として有名です。

121

Chapter 6

The present reality of Japanese/Korean relations
日韓問題の現実

The most peaceful and prosperous time in Korean history
歴史上最も平和で豊かだった時代

But was the Japanese annexation of Korea truly brutal, as many Western commentators state? They always use the word brutal, but then do not give any details.

多くの西洋人の解説者が言うように、日本の朝鮮併合は本当に残酷だったのでしょうか？

There was one violent demonstration during the Japanese annexation period. This was the March 1919 movement. Several hundred Koreans died in demonstrations across the country.

日本が併合している時代、1919年3月に暴動が起きました。この暴動により、朝鮮全域で、数百人の朝鮮人が死亡しました。

Until that time, Japanese administrators were former military men. After the demonstration, this was changed to civilians, and the type of government changed. For example, before the March 1919 movement, school teachers had military uniforms and wore swords.

それ以前、朝鮮総督は元軍人でしたが、暴動の後、総督武官制が廃止され、行政も変わりました。たとえば1919年3月の暴動前には、学校の先生は軍服姿でサーベルを下げていました。

第6章　日韓問題の現実

This was abandoned, in favor of civilian dress. And there were no more riots of any great size, or demonstrations under Japanese rule. If the critics are correct, that Japanese rule was brutal, Korea should have been seething with revolution.

その後、学校の先生は平服を着ました。それ以降、日本統治の間に大きな暴動は起こりませんでした。もし今も日本を批判している解説者の言うことが正しいのなら、そして日本の統治が本当に残酷なものだったのなら、当時の朝鮮で繰り返し暴動が起きていたでしょう。

It was not. There were constant riots before the Japanese annexation during the Yi dynasty, casualties in the tens of thousands, hundreds of thousands were common.

しかしそうではありませんでした。朝鮮併合前には頻繁に暴動があり、何万、何十万という死者が出るのが当たり前でした。

In a 1948 revolt across South Korea, President Rhee Syngmun killed 60,000 in Cheju island alone.

1948年に韓国で全国的に起きた暴動で、李承晩大統領は済州島だけで6万人を殺害しました。

Japan subdued Korea's guerillas
朝鮮人ゲリラを抑えた日本

During the Korean war, guerrillas fought in the south until 1956. They were both local guerrillas and remnants of the North Korean People's Army that had driven south in 1950.

朝鮮戦争の間、1956年までゲリラが韓国内で戦闘していました。

123

Chapter6 The present reality of Japanese/Korean relations

戦闘していたのは、1950 年に韓国に攻め込んだ北朝鮮軍の残党と、
韓国内のゲリラです。

Yet there were no active guerrillas at all in Korea throughout the
annexation period. There were two resistance forces that I know of. There
was a guerrilla group in Manchuria. They never numbered more than 1,500.
In a memoir by one of their members, "A North Korean remembers", he
described one of their forays into Korea proper. He said that they did not
dare approach a farmhouse for food or help even in the most remote areas.

それでも併合時代には、朝鮮全域で活動しているゲリラはいませ
んでした。私の知っている限りでは、二つのゲリラグループがあり
ました。満洲に一つのグループがあり、最も人数が多い時で 1,500
人程度でした。そのグループの一人の手記「北朝鮮は記憶している」
で、彼は当時朝鮮に侵入した話を書いています。辺鄙な地域の農家
でも、朝鮮人ゲリラは食料提供などの協力には絶対応じてもらえな
かったそうです。

The reason was that the farmer would inform the governmental police.
Now critics of Japan here will say that this was because the Japanese
police were too brutal, the people were afraid.

その農家は警察に通報しました。ここで、日本に批判的な解説者
は、日本の警察が残虐で、民衆は怖かったからだと言います。

No. Guerrilla war is people's war, it does not work like that. You cannot
destroy the will of people to fight by force.

違います。ゲリラ戦は人民の戦争ですから、そんなことはありま
せん。人民の戦う意志を、力ずくで奪うことはできません。

Let us take a quick look at the US effort in the Vietnam war. The United
States Army had some 9 divisions in Vietnam, plus one Marine division.
There were also some 13 South Vietnamese divisions plus other troops.

124

第 6 章　日韓問題の現実

Yet they could never eliminate resistance in Southern Vietnam. Eventually the Americans withdrew, abandoning the South Vietnamese government.

　ベトナム戦争を見てみましょう。アメリカはベトナムに陸軍 9 個師団、海兵隊 1 個師団を投入し、南ベトナム軍は 13 個師団その他が配備されていました。しかし、これだけの大軍でも、南ベトナムでの抵抗を排除することは不可能でした。結局、数年後にアメリカは撤退し、南ベトナム政府は見捨てられました。

A US division is about 20,000 men.

　アメリカの 1 個師団は約 2 万人です。

The number of Japanese Imperial Army troops in Korea during the annexation period was at most one or two divisions. A Japanese division at the time was about 10,000 men. If Korea was in constant revolt, a force of something like 10 to 15 divisions would have been required to keep order. As we have seen in Mr. Ireland's book, there was a slight majority of Japanese to Korean police in Korea in 1922. But as time went on, the number of ethnic Koreans increased in the police.

　併合時代の朝鮮半島にいた日本陸軍は 1 〜 2 個師団だけでした。当時、日本の師団は 1 万人ほどでした。もし当時の朝鮮半島で頻繁に暴動が起きていたら、秩序を維持するのに 10 個から 15 個師団が必要だったでしょう。アイルランド氏の本を読むと、1922 年の朝鮮の警察は、朝鮮人より日本人の数の方が多かったようです。しかし時間と共に、朝鮮人の警官の数が多くなりました。

If there had been people's war in Korea, a revolt against Japanese rule, most of these ethnic Korean police would have taken their weapons and run to the mountains.

　もし当時、朝鮮人民が日本支配に対して反乱を起こした場合、この朝鮮人の警官のほとんどは武器を所持したまま山へ逃げたでしょう。

125

Chapter6 The present reality of Japanese/Korean relations

If we look at a map, we can see that Korea is rather larger geographically than South Vietnam. Korea also has terrain ideally suited for guerrilla warfare. It has many rugged mountains.

地図を見れば、南ベトナムより当時の朝鮮の方が広いことが分かります。朝鮮半島の地勢を見ると、岩山が多く、ゲリラ戦にとても適しています。

If the Korean people did not acquiesce with Japanese rule, they would have taken to the mountains and fought. They had many times in the past, even with inferior weapons, fought with Yi dynasty government troops.

もし朝鮮の人々が日本統治に不満があったら、山にこもって戦ったでしょう。昔の朝鮮人は、劣った武器で、李氏朝鮮の軍と戦っていました。

This did not happen. This was because the overwhelming majority of Korean people saw Japanese rule as a chance for a better life.

しかし、そんなことは起こりませんでした。圧倒的多数の朝鮮人は、日本統治の方が良い生活ができることを理解していたからです。

America could not provide that in Vietnam, so their effort failed.

アメリカはベトナムで日本のようなことができず、南ベトナムの維持は失敗に終わりました。

There was also another Korean Resistance Army based in Shanghai, but they never numbered more than 100 men or so.

上海にもう一つ朝鮮人の抗日組織がありましたが、その数はたった 100 人程度でした。

Yet, I read articles where President Park Guen Hye demands that Japan apologize for the resistance fighters killed fighting Japan.

126

第6章　日韓問題の現実

　にもかかわらず、韓国の朴槿恵大統領が、日本と戦った抗日兵士への謝罪を、日本に要求しているというマスコミの記事を読んだことがあります。

There weren't any such soldiers. Sorry to Korean people, but that is the truth. There was never any guerrilla fighting inside Korea whatsoever against the annexation to Japan. The Japanese annexation was the most peaceful and prosperous time in Korean history.

　そんな兵士は存在していませんでした。韓国人にとっては残念ですが、それが真実です。併合時代、朝鮮半島でゲリラ戦は全くありませんでした。日本の併合時代は朝鮮の歴史の中で最も平和で、豊かな時代だったのです。

In 1910 when Japan annexed Korea, the population was 13,128,780 people. In 1942, it was 25,525,409 people. Under Japanese rule, the population doubled. If the Japanese military was constantly raiding Korean villages for women, and there was constant imprisonment and torture of Korean people as some people claim, the doubling of the population could not have happened.

　1910年の併合時、朝鮮の人口は13,128,780人でしたが、1942年には25,525,409人に増えています。日本の統治で、人口が倍になったのです。もし日本軍が慰安婦にするためにしょっちゅう村の女性を強制連行したり、頻繁に朝鮮人を刑務所で拷問にかけていたら、当時の朝鮮の人口は絶対に倍にはなりません。

The Korean victimhood syndrome
韓国人の被害者意識

Why do Koreans hate Japan so much? I lived in Korea in the late 1970's.

127

Chapter6 The present reality of Japanese/Korean relations

I remember a conversation I had with Korean friends one day. They asked me which country had the most difficult time in WWII.

　どうして韓国人はそれほどまでに日本を憎んでいるのでしょうか？　私は 1970 年代後半に、韓国に住んでいました。ある日の、韓国人の友人たちとの会話を覚えています。彼らは、「第二次世界大戦でどこの国が最もつらい経験をしたと思うか？」と私に尋ねました。

Well, I thought that it was a very unusual question, in the year 1978. I answered Poland. Poland was invaded by both Germany and Russia. The German occupation lasted some 6 years, and yes, it was harsh. There were two great revolts in Poland, the Jewish Warsaw uprising of 1943, and the Polish guerrilla Home Army revolt of 1944.

　1978 年のことでしたが、どうしてそんなことを聞くのかなと思いました。私はポーランドだと答えました。ポーランドはドイツとロシアの両方から侵略されました。ドイツの占領は 6 年間でしたが、それは本当に過酷なものでした。そのドイツ占領期間に二度、大きな武装蜂起が発生しています。1943 年のワルシャワ・ゲットー蜂起と 1944 年の抵抗組織ポーランド国内軍によるワルシャワ蜂起がありました。

Both were crushed totally. And as the Russian army advanced westward, the German Army fought tenaciously. All in all 25% of Polish people died int the war.

　どちらの蜂起も徹底的に鎮圧されました。その後、ロシア軍が徐々に西へと進撃し、ドイツ軍はポーランドに留まって頑強に戦いました。その結果、25％ものポーランド人の命が奪われました。

But when I said this, my Korean friends got very angry, and threatened me with violence. They screamed that Korea had the most difficult time in

128

第6章　日韓問題の現実

WWII. They were no longer my friends.And these Korean people insulted the people of Poland.

しかし、私がこの話をすると、その韓国人の友人たちは激怒して、私に殴りかからんばかりの勢いで威圧してきました。第二次世界大戦では、韓国が一番大変だったんだと叫びました。彼らとはもう友達の縁を切りました。この韓国人たちはポーランド人に対してとても失礼です。

But this illustrates part of the inferiority/superiority complex that Koreans have.

しかしこれで、韓国人が持つ、劣等感・優越感がよく分かります。

The Korean superiority complex
韓国人の優越感

They have a huge superiority complex. They insist that Korea is the center of the world, that Seoul is the best place in the universe. Everything in the world began in Korea.

彼らはとてつもない優越感を持っています。韓国が世界の中心、ソウルが大宇宙の中で一番素晴らしい所だと力説します。世界の文明も発明も何もかも韓国が起源だと言います。

When I lived in Korea, Koreans would often demand to me that America adopt the Hangul writing system, because it is the best in the world. Well, for them it is OK, but I grew up with the Roman alphabet in America. It works well for America. I now live in Japan, and read and write using the Japanese phonetic alphabets and Chinese characters.

私が韓国に住んでいた時に、韓国人が、よく私にアメリカはハン

129

Chapter6 The present reality of Japanese/Korean relations

グルを採用せよと要求してきました。世界でハングルが最も素晴らしい文字だからだそうです。まあ、韓国人にはハングルが良いと思いますが、私はアメリカでアルファベットで育ちました。アメリカでは、アルファベットが良いでしょう。私は今日本に住んでいますので、漢字、ひらがな、カタカナを使っています。

Another example is pizza. I watched this develop. In Korea, there is a dish called chijimi. It is made by frying vegetables, seafood or meat in batter, and produces a flat pancake like dish.

もう一つ、ピザの話があります。私はこの話の成り行きを知っています。韓国にはチヂミという料理があります。小麦粉に卵を混ぜた生地に野菜、シーフード、肉を加えて焼いたもので、見た目は皿のように平らな、パンケーキのような料理です。

When I lived in Korea it was described to foreigners as Korean pizza. Over the years, this story has morphed into, "Marco Polo stole the concept of pizza from Korea!"

私が韓国に住んでいた時に、この料理は「コリアンピザ」だと外国人に説明しました。しかし何年か経つうちに、この話は、「マルコ・ポーロが李氏朝鮮に来た時にチヂミからピザのアイデアを盗んだ！」になってしまいました。

Well, Marco Polo never visited Korea. But here we see this concept in the Korean mind that they are the victim. Somebody did some terrible wrong to them.

マルコ・ポーロは李氏朝鮮を訪問したことはありませんでした。でもこの話で、韓国人の「自分たちは犠牲者！」という意識がはっきり分かります。もし誰かが韓国人にひどいことをした場合、韓国人は永遠に自分が被害者だと考えます。

There are Koreans who also claim to have founded the Egyptian and

第 6 章　日韓問題の現実

Sumerian civilizations. They claim this because ancient texts say that Korea used to extend 40,000 ri (one ri is about 4 kilometers) from east to west.

　エジプト文明とシュメール文明は、昔朝鮮人が創設したと主張している韓国人がいます。古文書に、昔の朝鮮は東西４万里に及んでいたと書かれているからだそうです（１里は約４キロです）。

Well, when the ancients wrote things, they wrote to make the king look good. They exaggerated, modern day historians understand this.

　古代の人が、王の偉大さを誇張して書くことがあることを、現代の歴史家は理解しています。

Koreans also claim the rights to Christmas trees around the world. The Korean National Institute of Biological Resources has said that DNA studies prove that the trees used for Christmas trees around the world originated in Korea. And that they should be paid copyright fees whenever they are used.

　世界中で飾られているクリスマスツリーの権利を主張している韓国人もいます。韓国の生物資源研究所による遺伝子の分析で、世界のクリスマスツリーの起源は韓国であることが分かったということです。なので、クリスマスツリーを使う時には、韓国政府に著作権料を支払うべきであると言っています。

So every year when the President of the United States lights up the National Christmas Tree in front of the White House, will Korea send a bill?

　それでは、毎年、ホワイトハウスの前で、アメリカの大統領がナショナル・クリスマスツリーに点灯する度に、韓国政府は請求書を送ってくるのでしょうか？

131

Chapter6 The present reality of Japanese/Korean relations

This is another unfortunate Korean trait, making wild baseless historical claims, and then demanding money. This is characteristic of the Japanese/Korean relationship.

はっきりした根拠のない歴史的主張をして、お金を要求する。これがもう一つの韓国人の残念な特性です。そういうことが日本と韓国の間でよく見られます。

Examining the Comfort women issue
慰安婦問題を検証する

Let us look at some of the things that Koreans say happened during Japanese rule. First of all the Comfort Women issue.

それでは、韓国人が日本統治時代に日本が行ったと主張していることを見ていきましょう。まず、慰安婦問題です。

Koreans say that some 200,000 women were dragged from their villages, from the arms of wailing relatives, by Japanese Imperial Army troops. They were then taken to military brothels where they were forced to have sex with as many as 40 men a day.

韓国人の話ではこうです。日本陸軍の部隊が朝鮮全域の村々で、泣き叫ぶ家族の元から 200,000 人の女性を無理やり拉致しました。そして、その女性たちは軍専用の売春宿へ強制連行され、1 日に 40 人もの男たちとのセックスを強要されました。

If girls disobeyed, they were rolled naked across beds of nails, and boiled. The other girls were forced to eat them by Japanese soldiers.

もしその女性が命令に従わない場合、釘が飛び出した板の上を裸のまま転がされ、そして死ぬまでゆでられました。他の女性たちは、

第6章　日韓問題の現実

日本兵にその肉を食べるよう強要されました。

This is total fantasy. The Japanese Imperial Army never ever went into Korean villages. Internal order in Korea was basically kept by police. As we have seen, in 1922, in statistics provided by Alleyne Ireland in his work "The New Korea", nearly half of the police in Korea were ethnic Koreans.

これは完全なファンタジーです。日本陸軍の部隊は村に侵入していません。朝鮮国内の秩序は基本的に警察が守っていました。アレン・アイルランド氏の本「The New Korea」の統計によると、1922 年の時点で警察官の約半数は朝鮮人でした。

As time went on, this percentage increased until the majority of police under Japanese rule were ethnic Koreans. If the police, who were in fact Koreans, actually did enter villages and drag off young women, the people did not resist?

時間が経つにつれ、朝鮮人の警察官の数が増えて、大多数の警察官は朝鮮人になりました。警察官が（その多くは朝鮮人ですが）、村に侵入して女性を強制連行しても、村の人々は抵抗しないのでしょうか？

There was only one significant nation wide riot under Japanese rule, the March 1919 incident. Under Yi dynasty rule, and since then in post war Korea, violent protests were common. So why didn't the Korean people violently resist the Japanese government?

日本統治時代では、大きな暴動は一つだけ、1919 年 3 月の事件しかありませんでした。李氏朝鮮時代、そして大東亜戦争後、韓国では暴力的な抗議運動はよく発生していました。それでは、どうして朝鮮人は日本政府には抵抗しなかったのでしょうか。

Some Western fans of Korea might say that Japanese were horribly violent people. But if Koreans were terrified of Japan and were timid pussy

133

Chapter6 The present reality of Japanese/Korean relations

cats, yet before and after Japanese rule were ferocious tigers? This does not make sense. I know Korean people, believe me, they would fight if such a horrible thing, the kidnapping of women, happened in their village.

韓国を支持する西洋人は、「日本人が恐ろしく暴力的な国民だから」と言うかもしれません。しかし、日本統治の時代は朝鮮人は臆病な猫ちゃんなのに、その前後の期間は、獰猛な虎だったのでしょうか？ それでは筋が通りません。私は韓国人を理解しています。もし自分の村で女性が拉致されたら、彼らは戦いますよ！

Many foreigners, particularly American feminist activists, focus on the issue of coercion in the Comfort Women issue. They condemn prostitution, and apply standards of today to the issue.

多くの外国人、特にアメリカのフェミニスト活動家は、慰安婦問題では、強制性を中心に問題視しています。売春業を非難して、現在の価値基準をそのまま昔に適用しています。

Well it was fact that in both Japan and Korea at that time, a father could and often did sell a pretty daughter into prostitution due to poverty. In Japan, this practice no longer exists, and is forbidden by law. There is a thriving sex industry in Japan, but it is totally voluntary, and is monitored by the police.

まあ、当時日本でも朝鮮でも、貧困が原因で、父親は家族のために娘を売ることがありました。現在の日本ではもうありません、法律で禁止されています。日本には大きなセックス産業がありますが、女性がその業界に入るのは自分の意志であり、違法行為は警察が取り締まっています。

Korean prostitutes and US troops
米兵と韓国人売春婦

第6章　日韓問題の現実

I have visited a Comfort Women station in Korea in 1977. It was outside the American Air Force base of Kunsan, in southwest Korea. The name of the area was Silvertown. It was in the middle of rice fields, surrounded by high walls, with a guarded gate.

私は 1977 年に韓国の慰安所へ行ったことがあります。韓国南西の群山米空軍基地の外にありました。その慰安所は「Silvertown」と呼ばれていました。周りは田んぼで、周囲を高い壁で囲まれていて、門は警備されていました。

The gate was guarded by a Korean government security guard, and a uniformed, armed US Air Force military police man. US Air Force medical officers checked the girls for sexual diseases. But this made sense. Before the establishment of Silvertown, US military personnel would hunt for sex in drinking places in the town. This led to much fighting and trouble with the local Korean people.

門の警備は韓国政府の警備員と、武装した米空軍の憲兵がいました。米空軍の軍医が、そこにいる女性の性病検査を行いました。しかし、この慰安所ができたことには重要な意味がありました。「Silvertown」が設立される前に、米兵は街の飲み屋でセックスの相手をあさっていました。それが原因で、地元の韓国人とよく喧嘩になり、トラブルが数多く発生しました。

Some girls were indeed prostitutes, but most in the city of Kunsan were not, drunken US military personnel did not differentiate. So to avoid trouble, Silvertown was established in an isolated area outside the city.

群山市には本当の売春婦もいましたが、ほとんどの女性はそうではありません。酔った米兵はそれを区別しませんでした。それで、トラブルを避けるために、街の郊外の孤立した場所に「Silvertown」が造られたのです。

135

Chapter6 The present reality of Japanese/Korean relations

And girls were still sold in Korea in the 1970's. If an American military man wanted to marry a Korean bar girl, he had to pay off her debt to the bar before the girl could leave the country. This is because the girls had been sold by their families.

1970年代、韓国では女性の人身売買がまだありました。米兵が韓国人の売春婦と結婚した場合、その女性が出国するためには、彼女の借金を、彼女が働くバーの主人に支払う必要がありました。その女性は家族に売られてきたからです。

Of course most Korean girls who married American military men were not prostitutes. But in America, all such Korean women who married American military men suffer extreme prejudice in the Korean communities in America.

もちろん、米兵と結婚した韓国女性が全て売春婦というわけではありません。しかし、アメリカでは米兵と結婚した韓国人女性全員が、アメリカのコリアンコミュニティーからひどい差別を受けています。

I can attest to the veracity of US military causing trouble with women. When I was based in Japan, I traveled much throughout Japan. At first, I would invite other Marines to go with me, but they would always grab some girl, by force, drag her to me and since I spoke Japanese, explain to her that she should have sex with him.

私は米兵がなぜ女性と問題を起こすのか、その真相を証言できます。私は米海兵隊員として来日した時に、日本のあちこちを旅しました。最初の頃は、他の海兵隊員を一緒に行こうと誘いました。するといつも、どこへ行っても、女性の手首を掴んで私の所まで引っ張ってきて、日本語ができる私に、自分とセックスするよう伝えてほしいと言ってきました。

136

I would pass over my English/Japanese dictionary and tell him to do it himself. So after a few bad experiences, I traveled alone in Japan.

私は自分の英和辞書を渡して、「自分で言え」と言いました。何度かそんな嫌な経験をしたので、一人で日本を旅しました。

American Feminists will not like this, but this is reality. This kind of thing has happened outside military camps since the dawn of humanity.

アメリカのフェミニストはこういうことは嫌いだと思います。でも、それが現実です。太古の昔から、軍のキャンプの周りでは、こういうことが起きているのです。

And such things still continue today. Girls who get into debt in Korea, for example with credit cards, are told there is one way to pay it off, become a prostitute overseas, in Japan, America, Australia or Europe.

現在でも同じような事が続いています。韓国でクレジットカードなどで借金を抱えた女性は、ヨーロッパ、オーストラリア、日本、アメリカで売春婦になれば返済できると言われます。

Today in the US, 24% of trafficked foreign women come from South Korea.

現在のアメリカにおける、人身売買された外国人女性の 24％は、韓国から来ています。

The truth of the Comfort Women issue
慰安婦問題の真実

But in Korea during the annexation to Japan, there were no forcible round ups of Korean women to be prostitutes. In fact there were open

Chapter6 The present reality of Japanese/Korean relations

advertisements in newspapers, detailing the salary to be expected. The pay for Comfort Women was extremely good, much better than the pay for Japanese enlisted troops.

　日本の併合時代、朝鮮の女性を強制連行して売春婦にするということはありませんでした。実は、新聞に広告が出され、給料がはっきり書かれていました。慰安婦の給料はとても良く、日本軍兵士よりはるかに高給でした。

There were ethnic Koreans who used deceptive methods to recruit prostitutes, but they were arrested and prosecuted by the Japanese government.

　詐欺的な方法で女性を集める朝鮮人がいましたが、日本政府によって逮捕、起訴されました。

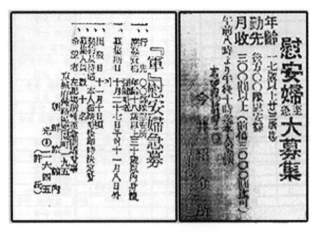

Newspaper advertisements for Comfort Women to work as prostitutes.

慰安婦募集の公告。朝鮮総督府機関誌「毎日新報」(左) と新聞「京城日報」。後者には月収 300 円以上 (前借 3000 円まで可) と書かれている。

第6章　日韓問題の現実

Comfort Women had home leave, and could socialize with Japanese troops in their free time. In fact, they had more privileges than American Comfort Women.

慰安婦は休暇で故郷に帰ったり、休みの日に日本兵と普通に付き合うこともできました。実際、アメリカの慰安婦より多くの特権がありました。

Yes, American did have an organized system of government sponsored prostitution. It was in Hawaii during WWII. The Hawaiian territorial government knew that when the war started, many drunken service men on their war to war would pass through Hawaii. They did not want these troops in the better parts of Honolulu, where their wives and daughters lived.

そうです。アメリカには政府出資の組織化された売春システムがあり、大東亜戦争の時にハワイで運営されていました。ハワイ準州政府は、戦争が始まれば、飲んだくれのアメリカ兵が大勢ハワイ経由で前線へ行くということを知っていたので、妻や娘がいる要職者が住むホノルルの優良な地域に、そんな米兵が来ることを警戒し、トラブルを回避する方法を検討しました。

So down near the port, "Hotel Street" was created. The US military, Hawaiian government, and Hawaiian police all cooperated in this effort. The hotels were already there. Being American, things were on an assembly line basis. The military man would go into the room, strip, and wash his private parts with disinfectant. The girl would come in, put a condom on the service man, and then he had 3 minutes.

それで、港の近くに「ホテルストリート」が作られました。これには米軍、ハワイ準州政府、ハワイ警察が協力しました。そのホテル街は以前からありました。そこでは工場の流れ作業のようなサービスが行われていました。兵士は部屋に入り、服を脱いで、消毒液

139

Chapter6 The present reality of Japanese/Korean relations

で自分の下半身を洗います。女性が部屋に入ってきて、兵士にコンドームを付け、それから3分でセックスを済ませます。

The military called these troops "3 minute men". They referred to hotel street as the area to get lubed, screwed, and tattooed. The American women would do 100 men a day.

こういう兵士のことを軍隊の俗語で「3分の男」と呼びました。ホテルストリートは「lubed, screwed, and tattooed」する所だと言われました。lubeは潤滑油をさす、つまりお酒を飲む、screwはセックスする、tattooedは刺青を入れる、という意味です。このアメリカの売春婦は1日に100人もの相手をしました。

US troops lining up outside an American Comfort Women establishment in Hawaii.
ホノルルの売春宿が並ぶホテルストリートで行列する米海軍の水兵たち。

第6章　日韓問題の現実

They made a lot of money, but the labor conditions were strict. They could not own a house or car, and could not leave the area of hotel street. Most of these women were professional prostitutes from San Francisco.

売春婦たちはかなりのお金を儲けましたが、労働条件は厳しいものでした。車も家も買うことを禁止され、ホテルストリートの区域から出ることも禁止されていました。この女性たちはほとんどがサンフランシスコから来たプロの売春婦でした。

Many Japanese and ethnic Comfort Women did have contracts that they were obligated to serve out. Their families had received money from brokers, it had to be paid back.

日本の慰安婦は、契約した期間、奉仕する義務がありました。慰安婦の家族は、ブローカーからお金を貰っていたので、それを返済しなければなりませんでした。

But the Japanese system was safe and clean. There was none of the brutality that Koreans say happened.

しかし、日本のシステムは安全で衛生的でした。韓国人が言うような虐待はありませんでした。

And today, the Korean former Comfort Women give very emotional heart wrenching performances. Yet I have read of people having witnessed the women, after the performance, coming around to the back entrance of the venue where the event was held, and being given envelopes of money.

現在、元韓国人慰安婦はとても感情的で痛ましいパフォーマンスを行っています。しかし、私が読んだ記事では、パフォーマンスが終わると、その元慰安婦たちはイベント会場の裏口で、お金が入った封筒をもらっている、ということでした。

And I have seen photos of the same women, sometimes she is in a

141

Chapter6 The present reality of Japanese/Korean relations

wheelchair, sometimes she walks just fine. This is a staged show, an act, designed to get the sympathy of Westerners who do not have much knowledge about recent Asian history.

　私も、ある時は車椅子、ある時は元気に歩いている、同じ女性の写真を見たことがあります。これは芝居で、東洋の歴史を知らない西洋人の同情を買うために演じています。

Did Japan destroy Korea's culture?
日本は本当に朝鮮の文化を破壊したのか？

Koreans also claim that Japan destroyed their culture. Well, Japan revived the Korean alphabet, the Yi dynasty Yangban had let it go out of use. The only education in Yi dynasty Korea was in Chinese.

　韓国人は日本が自分たちの文化を破壊したと主張しています。李氏朝鮮の両班がハングルを相手にせず、だんだん使われなくなりましたが、日本が統治時代にハングルを復興させました。李氏朝鮮の時代の教育は漢字のみでした。

When the the French colonized Vietnam, they discouraged the use of or banned Chu Nom, the Chinese ideograph based Vietnamese writing.

　フランスがベトナムを植民地にした時は、漢字に似たチュノムというベトナム文字の使用を禁止しました。

Vietnamese then embraced Roman letters. Today few can read the old Chu Nom texts. But unlike Koreans who always complain about Japan, Vietnamese do not roam the world crying about the French.

　ベトナム人は、ローマ字を受け入れました。現在、チュノムを読めるベトナム人はごくわずかです。でも、いつも日本に文句を言う

142

第6章　日韓問題の現実

韓国人とは異なり、ベトナム人は世界中でフランスの悪口を触れ回ったりしません。

If Japan had truly banned Hangul, after 35 years of annexation, almost nobody could read it in 1945 when Japan surrendered and Korea was transferred to the control of the United States and Soviet Russia. Yet at that time most Koreans were literate in Hangul and Japanese both.

もし日本が本当にハングルを禁止していたら、併合から35年後、日本が降伏して米ソが朝鮮を支配するようになった時に、ほとんどの朝鮮人がハングルを読めなかったでしょう。しかし、1945年当時の朝鮮人は日本語とハングルの両方を読めました。

It is Japan's creating a mass education system that was revolutionary in creating a Korea where all Koreans could prosper regardless of class, at least in post war South Korea.

日本は統治した朝鮮に、革新的な大衆教育システムを導入しました。これにより、朝鮮人は誰でも豊かな生活ができる可能性が生まれました。

I do know of one practice that Japan did ban during this period, which has been revived as a Korean folk dance today. This is the Byeongsin chum, or dance to mock the handicapped. I have problems with this. I have seen YouTube videos of this dance, I cannot find anything to admire here. The Wikipedia entry says that its purpose is to satirize the nobility. But the more you study Korea, the more you find a cruel streak in Korea society.

李氏朝鮮のある踊りが併合後に禁止されました。現在、北朝鮮と韓国で民族舞踊として復活しています。それは、病身舞という踊りです。この踊りは、体の不自由な人を嘲るものです。私はこの踊りが嫌いです。YouTubeで見ましたが、どこがいいのか分かりません。ウィキペディアでは、この踊りの本当の意味は貴族たちに対する風

143

Chapter6 The present reality of Japanese/Korean relations

刺である、と書いています。しかし、コリアを研究すると、コリア社会の残酷な面がいろいろと見えてきます。

Japan was correct to ban this practice.

日本がこの踊りを禁止したのは、正しいことでした。

Koreans also say that they were forced to speak Japanese. Well, since Korea was very hierarchal under the Yi Dynasty, it was natural that Japanese speaking Koreans would consider them selves superior to those who could not. This is part of the fabricated story of destroying Korean culture.

韓国人の話では、日本人から、日本語を使うよう強制されたと言います。まあ李氏朝鮮は非常に階級的な社会でしたから、併合時代の朝鮮で日本語ができる朝鮮人は、できない朝鮮人に対して優越感を持てたでしょう。これは、日本が朝鮮の文化を潰したという、嘘だらけの話の原因の一つです。

In the same way in Japan, in the post WWII American occupation and American dominance era. Japanese people who could speak English had much status in Japan. But that time is ending,and Japanese people are losing interest in America and speaking English.

日本も同じです。大東亜戦争後、アメリカの占拠時代とアメリカの日本支配時代、日本では英語を喋る人が威張っていました。しかし、その時代も終わり、だんだん日本人はアメリカや、英語を喋ることに興味を失っています。

In any case, Koreans certainly did not forget to speak Korean, so it must have been used on daily basis during the annexation. And the truth is most Japanese people who moved to Korea during that period, learned to speak Korean.

第6章　日韓問題の現実

　いずれにしても、当時の朝鮮人は当然朝鮮語ができるので、併合時代、毎日使っていたでしょう。そして、併合時代に朝鮮に住んでいた日本人のほとんどが、朝鮮語を学んでいたという事実があります。

The adoption of Japanese names
創氏改名の真実

Another big complaint of the Koreans is that Japan forced people to adopt Japanese names. No. It was voluntary.

　もう一つ、韓国人が強く訴えているのは、日本が朝鮮人に日本の名前を使うように強制した、というものです。違います。自由意志によるものでした。

But Koreans still use Japanese names today. Yes, in America. I have seen advertisements for massage parlors, which are really centers of Korean prostitution. They always use names like Sakura, Tokyo, Nagoya, Osaka or something.

　しかし、韓国人は現代でも日本の名前を使っています。アメリカでの話です。私は韓国系のマッサージパーラーの広告を見たことがありますが、実際はそこで売春が行われています。よく使われる店の名前は、さくら、東京、大阪、名古屋などです。

First of all, in Japanese, it comes off as tacky. But nowhere do I see a Korean massage parlor with a name like Seoul, Pusan, or Taegu. Why? Aren't the Korean people proud of their culture. Well, they have much pride, but also, a tremendous inferiority complex towards Japan.

　まず、日本語でこのように店に地名を付けるのはお洒落とは言えませんが、それにしても韓国のソウル、釜山、大邱という名前を使っ

145

Chapter6 The present reality of Japanese/Korean relations

ているマッサージパーラーを私は見たことがありません。韓国人は自分の文化に誇りがないのでしょうか？　まあ、誇りはあるのでしょうが、日本に対して、とても強い劣等感を持っているようです。

I have also seen Korean canned goods labeled with Japanese names like Geisha, or Sakura.

さくら、芸者などの名称をつけた韓国の缶詰も見たことがあります。

The Koreans claim that they are the source of Japanese culture
韓国人による文化・起源の主張

Koreans claim many aspects of Japanese culture originated in Korea. They claim Samurai came from the Saulabi, who were the original such warriors in the ancient Paekche kingdom. There is no evidence to support this.

韓国人はよく、日本の文化は韓国が起源だと主張しています。彼らは、日本の武士、侍の起源は、百済の「サウラビ」であると主張します。しかし証拠はありません。

They claim to have originated the Japanese tea ceremony. I have seen a video of a Korean tea ceremony, they use a metal thermos for the hot water. In Japan, that would be an incredible rudeness, no Japanese would perform it in that way.

韓国人は日本の茶道の起源も韓国だと言います。その韓国茶道のビデオを見たことがありますが、お湯は魔法瓶に入っていました。日本では、それは本当に失礼なことで、日本人は絶対にそのようなことをしません。

第6章　日韓問題の現実

And of course they claim that cherry trees, popular for viewing the spring flower blooms in Japan, originated from Korea.

それに日本のソメイヨシノ、春のお花見でも大人気ですが、彼らは、朝鮮半島が起源だと言います。

These cultural claims do make the Korean people unique, and not in a good way. It is a sign of mental illness, on a national scale. No other countries with a rivalry with another nation do such things.

このような主張をするのは、世界で韓国人だけです。しかしこれは良い話ではありません。国家規模の精神疾患の兆候です。他国とライバル関係にあるどの国だって、こんなことはやりません。

Fro example, The English have a great rivalry with the French. But any English person will freely admit that French cuisine is much superior to British. They will also say that the French language is more beautiful to the ear. I am a native speaker of English, and also a French speaker, I agree with this. And no English person would try to imitate and pass themselves off as French.

たとえば、英国人とフランス人は、昔から強力なライバル関係にあります。でも、英国人は、英国料理よりフランス料理の方が美味しいことを率直に認めますし、英語よりフランス語の方が綺麗に聞こえると言います。私は英語が母国語ですが、フランス語もできますので、この意見には同意します。しかし、英国人がフランス人を真似たり、なりすますようなことは絶対にしません。

Koreans in other countries all the time say they are Japanese.

韓国人は、他国でよく自分は日本人だと言います。

147

Chapter6 The present reality of Japanese/Korean relations

Rampant persecutions in the name of patriotism
「愛国無罪」の暴走

By far, not all Koreans have such feelings of hatred for Japan. But to express that concept can be dangerous. In 2013, in a park in South Korea, a 95 year old man was beaten to death by a man in his 30's. The reason was because the old man said that the Japanese annexation period benefited Korea. The young man said he felt uncontrollable anger, and killed him.

もちろん、全ての韓国人が日本に対して嫌悪感を持っているわけではありません。しかし、韓国国内で、そんな感情をはっきり出すのは危険です。2013 年にソウルの公園で、30 代の男性が 95 歳の男性を殴り殺しました。その老人が併合は韓国にとって良いことだったと言ったからです。その 30 代の男性は、怒りを抑えられず、その老人を殺してしまいました。

The judge said that the young man's actions were understandable, and gave him a 5 year sentence, very light for murder.

裁判官はその男性の犯行に到った動機は理解できると言い、懲役 5 年を宣告しました。殺人事件としては、非常に軽い刑でした。

I thought old people were respected in Korea, a country that treasures the teaching of Confucius.

私は、儒教の教えを大切にしている韓国の人々は、お年寄りを尊敬していると思っていました。

I have seen photos on the net, of a Seoul university professor being beaten and forced to bow in apology to the Comfort Women. The reason was because he said in his research, he could find no evidence of Japanese military or government coercion.

第6章　日韓問題の現実

ネットで、ソウル大学の教授が殴られ、元慰安婦の前で土下座を強要されている写真を見ました。その教授の調査では、日本政府・日本軍が慰安婦を強制連行した証拠は見つからなかった、と発言したのが原因でした。

I thought teachers were respected in Korea, a country that treasures the teaching of Confucius.

私は、儒教の教えを大切にしている韓国の人々は、学校の先生を尊敬していると思っていました。

I have heard many such stories about Korean friends of Japanese friends, that they fear for their lives in South Korea if they speak about Japan in a positive way.

他にも、韓国で日本のことを肯定的に話したら殺されかねないという話を、韓国人の友人がいる日本人からよく耳にします。

Korean actions have blowback
韓国人の自業自得

Anti Japanese sentiment is reaching a level of hysteria in Korea today. Those Comfort Women statues spreading around the world, they are beginning to look like some sort of cult.

今日、韓国の反日感情はヒステリーのレベルになっています。世界中に広がる慰安婦像は、まるでカルトのようです。

This has already had a very negative impact on Japanese Korean relations. Up until a few years ago, there was a Korean cultural boom in Japan. Korean dramas were popular on TV. K-pop stars, and Korean stars, had masses of Japanese fans.

149

Chapter6 The present reality of Japanese/Korean relations

　この問題が、日韓関係にとても悪い影響を及ぼしています。数年前まで、日本は韓流ブームでした。韓国のテレビドラマは日本で人気でしたし、K-POP スターや韓流映画スターが数多くの日本人ファンを獲得しました。

Many Japanese traveled to South Korea, to tour the area where those dramas were filmed. Korean food, and Korean language classes were popular in Japan.

　多くの日本人が、そのドラマロケ地を見に韓国に観光旅行していましたし、韓国料理、韓国語のクラスも日本で人気でした。

That is all over. The Korean hysteria over the Comfort Women issue, and nasty treatment of Japanese people has back fired. Now, Japanese tourists shun Korea as a destination, and their tourist industry is in collapse.

　それが急速に萎んでしまいました。韓国人の慰安婦問題におけるヒステリーと、日本人に対するひどい扱いが、この失敗に繋がりました。現在、日本人観光客が激減したため、韓国の観光業界は崩壊寸前です。

And the Korea people express bewilderment at this. Are they really that stupid? Apparently, due to their feelings of superiority, they felt that no matter how insulting they acted toward Japanese people, we would still come to Korea and spend money.

　韓国人はそのことに困惑しています。しかし、どうしてそうなったのか、分からないのでしょうか？　やはり、自分たちの方が上位であるという根拠のない優越感があり、日本人にはどんな失礼な態度をとっても、日本人はまた韓国へ観光にきて、お金を落とすと思っていたのでしょう。

What do I mean?

150

第6章　日韓問題の現実

この間、以下のような事件がありました。

In 2015, Mr Kato Tatsuya, of the Sankei newspaper, was forbidden to leave Korea. He was accused of defamation. His crime was to reprint an article, written by a Korean reporter, about the whereabouts of President Park during the Sewol ferry disaster. The Korean reporter was never charged with any crime.

2015年に、産経新聞の加藤達也さんが韓国から出国禁止の命令を受けました。名誉毀損で告発されたのです。その理由は、韓国人記者が韓国語で書いた記事を、翻訳して記事にしたことです。内容は、セウォル号フェリー転覆事故の時に、数時間朴槿恵大統領が所在不明だったというもので、元の記事を書いた韓国人記者は告発されませんでした。

But he was told by the Korean prosecution, that if he admitted to wrong doing, and paid a fine, he could leave Korea and return to Japan. I thought that this kind of shakedown only happened in kleptocratic third world countries.

加藤さんは韓国の検察から、悪いことをしたと認めて、罰金を払えば、韓国を出て日本に帰ることができると言われました。私は、このようなゆすり行為は、第三世界の腐敗した略奪国家でしか起こらないと思っていました。

Eventually after some time Mr. Kato was cleared of all charges.

数ヵ月後、一審で無罪判決が出され、韓国の検察は控訴を断念しました。

But these actions make Korea unpopular as a tourist destination.

しかし、こういう異常なことが次々起きたせいで、韓国はもう観光スポットとしての人気がなくなりました。

151

Chapter6 The present reality of Japanese/Korean relations

And now the Korean tourist industry is near collapse. Korea is descending into rule of the thug.

韓国の観光業はまもなく崩壊するでしょう。韓国は悪党が支配する社会に成り下がっています。

The Korean poop fetish
韓国人の「大便フェチ」

In fact, Korean people seem to be de-evolving, regressing. They are becoming infantile. I think it is now time to write about the poop fetish.

実際に、韓国人は退化しているように見えますし、幼稚になっています。それでは、これから大便フェチについて書いていきしょう。

Now it may surprise you that I bring up such a subject in a book like this. What the truth is, South Koreans are infatuated with feces. There is a cafe in central Seoul called Ddong cafe, with all kinds of goods, like pooping dolls, toilet plungers, and toilets throughout the establishment.

読者の皆さんは、このような話題を書くことに驚かれるかもしれません。しかし本当に、韓国人は大便が大好きです。ソウルの中心に、Ddong カフェという所があります。店のあちこちに、大便をしている人形、トイレ用吸引カップ、便器をモチーフにした作品など様々なグッズがあります。

They sell ddongbang, poop shaped pastries. There is a popular character in Korean culture called Dongchimee, which translates as "Poop man". And the Poop Man doll is capable of performing the act of defecation. There is also a girl doll that does the same thing.

店では、ddongbang という大便の形をした菓子を売っています。

第6章　日韓問題の現実

Dongchimee という韓国の人気キャラクターの商品もありますが、それは大便男という意味です。その大便男の人形は排便することができます。同様の女の子の人形もあります。

South of Seoul, in the city of Suwon there is a museum that is dedicated to toilet affairs that has many statues of people in the act of defecation. There are also smaller museums across the country.

ソウルの南の水原市にあるトイレ博物館には、排便中の人物の像がたくさんあります。規模はそれより小さいですが、韓国中に同じテーマの博物館があります。

And it is not only in museums that this poop fetish exists. Teekwondo is considered the national martial art of Korea. This year, some Taekwondo competitor was dissatisfied with a ruling by the Taekwondo council, and scattered feces and urine in the Taekwondo office building hallway before a major event.

この大便フェチは博物館だけの話ではありません。テコンドーは韓国の国技です。今年、テコンドー国技院の理事選出に不満があったテコンドー関係者が、理事会が開催される時に、国技院の廊下に糞尿をまき散らしました。

Now, I cannot imagine an athlete from any other country doing such a thing.

他の国で、スポーツ関係者がそんなことをするなど想像できません。

153

Chapter6 The present reality of Japanese/Korean relations

The Korean cult of bashing Japan
韓国人の日本バッシング

Now South Korea is a country where its people have made a religion of attacking Japan. Comfort Women statues appear everywhere. I have seen photos of people speaking in Korea in front of Comfort Women statues over 5 meters in size.

　韓国では日本バッシングは宗教になっています。慰安婦像はどこでもありますし、韓国で5メートルもの慰安婦像の前で人がスピーチしている写真を見たことがあります。

The Comfort Women issue has become some kind of weird religion.

　慰安婦問題は、怪しげな宗教になっています。

In Seoul, the old city hall built in the Japanese annexation era, was too small, a new one had to be built. Many anti-Japanese South Koreans wanted to destroy it as a symbol of Japan, but other Koreans wanted to preserve it for its historical significance.

　ソウルの市庁舎は、併合時代に建設されたもので小さかったので、新しい庁舎が必要でした。多くの反日的な韓国人は、その建物は日本のシンボルだから解体したいと思っていましたが、歴史的重要性のある建物なので、残すべきであると考える韓国人もいました。

They won, and a new town hall was built behind it. However, it was built in the shape of a giant wave about to destroy the old building.

　残すべきと考える人たちの意見が通り、新庁舎は旧庁舎の裏に建設されることになりました。しかし、新庁舎は、巨大な波が今にも旧庁舎を飲み込むかのような形だったのです。

第6章　日韓問題の現実

In March of 2011 Japan suffered a terrible earthquake. Korean people celebrated this, calling it the punishment of heaven.

2011年3月に、日本で恐ろしい地震が発生しました。韓国人はこの災害を祝い、そして、天罰だと言いました。

But Koreans are not only nasty towards Japan. I remember the 2002 World Cup. Not only was the cheating and bribery by Korea massive, but their manners were atrocious.

しかし、韓国人は日本だけに卑劣なわけではありません。2002年のワールドカップを覚えています。これは大がかりな不正行為と賄賂の問題だけでなく、一般の韓国人のマナーも最悪でした。

I remember seeing a banner about 20 meters long, with "Go to hell" written in Italian during the Korean match against Italy. I think 5 obvious goals by the Italian team were disqualified by the bribed judge.

韓国対イタリアの試合では、20メートルの横断幕に、イタリア語で「地獄へ行け！」と書かれていました。その試合の審判は賄賂をもらっていたのだと思いますが、5つぐらいの明らかなイタリアのゴールを無効にしました。

I also remember seeing on TV vendors outside the stadium before the match against Germany. They were selling photos of the German team members with black funerary ribbons on them, a tremendous insult.

ドイツとの試合の前に、スタジアムの外にある売店がテレビに映りました。ドイツチームのメンバーの写真を販売していましたが、その写真は遺影のように黒いリボンを付けて売っていました。これは呆れるほど失礼なことです。

In almost any sporting event involving a Japanese team in South Korea, there is cheating involved. In a badminton match, the competing teams

155

Chapter6 The present reality of Japanese/Korean relations

switch sides half way through. Well in the stadium in Korea, blowers had been installed that blew against the Japanese, no matter which side of the net they were on.

　日本対韓国のスポーツの試合が韓国で行われる場合、たいてい韓国サイドから何らかの不正行為があります。バドミントンの試合では、途中でコートチェンジを行います。しかし、その韓国の体育館では、コートのどちら側でも、日本側に強い向かい風が吹く空調操作が行われました。

But cheating is not limited to sports. I saw a video on YouTube, about a sweets contest World Championship held in Switzerland in 2010. Among the 5 finalists creating fantastic desserts were teams from South Korea and Japan.

　不正行為はスポーツの世界だけではありません。YouTube で、2010 年にスイスで行われたスウィーツ世界大会の映像を見ました。豪華で素晴らしいデザートを作る 5 組の決勝戦出場チームの中に、韓国と日本チームがいました。

The Korean team leader boasted on camera how he would not let Japan beat them. But their cheating was spotted. The Korean team shared a freezer with the Japanese team. The Koreans kept the freezer door open for long lengths of time, so that the Japanese desert partially melted.

　韓国のチームリーダーが、カメラの前で日本には勝たせないと自慢げに話をしていました。しかし、韓国側に不正行為が見られました。日本チーム、韓国チームは同じ冷蔵庫を使っていましたが、韓国チームは、わざと長い時間冷蔵庫のドアを開けていたため、日本チームが作ったデザートが一部溶けてしまったのです。

The South Korean team was penalized. But the Japanese team made a little chocolate cup, which poured molten chocolate over the ruined desert,

156

第6章　日韓問題の現実

and won the contest.

　韓国チームは警告を受けました。しかし、それでも日本チームは、そのデザートに、小さなカップから温かいチョコレートソースを注ぐ斬新なアイデアもあって、優勝しました。

But Korean people, do you really have to cheat at badminton and in a dessert contest?

　しかし、韓国の皆さん、デザート世界大会やバドミントンの試合のように、相手が日本人なら不正をしても良いのだと、本当に思っているのですか？

Anti Japanese Korean education
韓国における反日教育

The Korean education system teaches hatred of Japan, and a glorification of Korea's role in the Pacific war. Koreans are taught that they were one of the Allied powers, when the truth is that they enthusiastically fought for Japan.

　韓国の教育システムでは、日本に対する憎しみと、大東亜戦争でのコリアの役割を美化して教えています。学校では、コリアは連合国の一つであると教えられますが、実際は、併合時代の朝鮮人は、日本人として日本のために一生懸命勇敢に戦いました。

Well they were Japanese citizens at the time, present day Koreans are ashamed of this.

　併合時代は、当時朝鮮にいた人たちは皆日本国民でした。現在の韓国人はこの事実を恥じています。

Chapter6 The present reality of Japanese/Korean relations

I have seen a Japanese TV broadcast. They went into a Korean primary school. The lesson being taught was that the leader of North Korea, Kim Jong Il, was good man working for reunification.

少し前のことですが、韓国の小学校を訪問する日本のテレビ番組を見ました。その日の授業は、金正日という北朝鮮のリーダーは、統一のために努力している良い人だという内容でした。

The teachers openly said in the interview that this was necessary to prepare for reunification.

インタビューで、韓国の学校の先生が、この教育は統一の準備のために必要であると話していました。

I have seen on YouTube videos of Korean primary school students making paintings. The teachers encourage them. The paintings show Japan on fire, Japan sinking. They were all terrible. Children at that age do not think of such things naturally. They are being taught to hate.

YouTube で、韓国人の小学生が絵を描いている映像を見たことがあります。先生たちが生徒を励ましています。そこには、日本が燃えている、あるいは沈没している絵が描かれています。全部恐ろしい絵でした。その年齢の子供が自然にそのようなことを考えるわけがありません。学校が日本を憎むよう教育しているからです。

The fact is, this is nothing resembling any truth. Korean educators teach for ideological reasons, not to teach truth. So it is with the anti-Japan education.

韓国の教育者は真実を教えるのではなく、イデオロギーのために嘘を教えています。反日教育もそうです。

And this anti-Japan education has produced people who take action against Japan.

158

第6章　日韓問題の現実

　この反日教育は、日本に対して行動を起こす人をたくさん生み出しました。

Koreans are jealous of Japanese culture, they want to destroy it. I have seen videos on the net of Koreans defacing books in a public library.

　韓国人は日本の文化を妬んでいて、それらを崩壊させたいようです。ネット上のビデオで、韓国人が図書館にある本を改竄しているものを見ました。

In December of 2015 a Korean man planted a bomb inside a restroom at Yasukuni shrine in Tokyo. The bomb only partially exploded. He was arrested when he came back for a second try. In court, he said his motive was to become a famous hero in South Korea.

　2015 年 12 月に、韓国人男性が靖国神社のトイレに爆弾を仕掛けました。爆弾は不発でしたが、その犯人が、再度爆弾を設置しようと日本に入国した時に逮捕されました。裁判で、彼は韓国で英雄になりたいという動機から、爆弾を設置したと述べました。

Vandalism of public library books, and setting bombs are crimes. What kind of country is it where committing a crime makes you a hero?

　図書館の本を書き換える行為、爆弾設置は全て犯罪です。犯罪者が英雄になるとは、一体どういう国なんですか？

But is not this jealousy the true reason for Korean hatred of Japan? Japanese culture is renowned the world over. The tale of Genji. Kabuki, Noh. Kyoto is an exquisite city. I have also been to Kyongju in Korea, but it just does not compare to Kyoto. And many other cities in Japan are indeed beautiful.

　しかし、この嫉妬心が、韓国人が日本を憎悪する本当の理由ではないでしょうか？　世界中で日本の文化が尊敬されています。源氏

159

物語は有名ですし、歌舞伎、能楽は魅力があります。京都は非常に美しい街です。韓国の慶州市に行ったことがありますが、比較になりません。そして、その他の日本の街も綺麗な所が多いです。

Well, why is this? It is because of the nature of Yi dynasty Korea, a top down society where only the very elite could read. That is why a deep Korean culture could never really develop. To the Korean mind, thinking with a background of Confucianism, Japan must be an inferior barbarian nation in all respects.

これはなぜでしょうか？　李氏朝鮮時代の専制社会では、文字を読むことができたのはエリートだけでした。それで、朝鮮の文化が深まることはありませんでした。儒教が根付いた韓国人の考えでは、日本はあらゆる点で劣った野蛮人の国でなければなりません。

Yet the truth is in every way, Japan outshines Korea. And the best, most prosperous period in Korean history was under Japanese rule. This infuriates the Koreans.

しかし実際は、あらゆる点で日本は韓国より優れています。そして、コリアの歴史の中で、一番平和で、豊かな時代は日本統治時代でした。この事実は、韓国人を激怒させます。

"Korean fatigue" among foreigners
外国人の「韓国疲れ」

If Koreans kept this irrational hate merely to themselves, it might not be such an issue. But Korean people are traveling the world, peddling false stories that Japan was so terrible to them.

もし韓国人が、その反日感情を内輪だけで留めていれば、大した問題ではなかったのかもしれません。しかし韓国人は世界中で日本

第6章　日韓問題の現実

がコリアにひどいことをした、という嘘をまき散らしています。

This Comfort Women statue has become the symbol of some sort of weird religion. In photos, I see people covering the statue in Seoul with scarves and caps in the winter time. That is a form of worship. It is a totally exaggerated story, and Koreans look rather ridiculous.

　慰安婦像はおかしな宗教のシンボルになっています。冬、ソウルの慰安婦像に、帽子がかぶせられ、スカーフが巻かれているのを写真で見ました。これは崇拝です。韓国人が滑稽に見えます。

And the reception Koreans get from foreigners. Well, at first they got sympathy. After all, very few Westerners understand the truth of WWII. But gradually, they get tired of constant Korean stories about how bad Japan is.

　それでは、外国人は韓国人の話をどのように受け止めているのでしょうか？　最初は、同情しました。第二次世界大戦の真実を知っている西洋人は少ないですから。しかし、韓国人があまりに「日本はひどい！」という話を繰り返すものだから、だんだんウンザリしてきています。

The thing is, Koreans are not doing anything to help their country themselves, they are asking foreigners to attack Japan for them. This entire anti-Japan international effort is to seek foreign help for Korea to dominate Japan.

　問題は、韓国人は自分の国のために、自分で努力して何とかしようとせず、外国人の力を借りて日本を攻撃していることです。この国際的な韓国の反日活動は、韓国が日本より優位に立つために、外国人を利用しようというものです。

There is a word appearing now in Western writings about Korea, it is called Korea fatigue. They are getting tired of constant complaints about

161

Japan.

韓国について西洋人が書いた本にこういう言葉があります。「韓国疲れ」というものです。外国人は、執拗に繰り返される日本批判に疲れています。

Personal memories of Korea
韓国に対する私の思い

Some people may wonder why I am so critical of Korea, but I have a right. I can say I fought for their country.

なぜ私がこんなに韓国に対して批判的なのかと思う人がいるかもしれません。しかし、私にはその権利があります。私は韓国のために戦ったと言えるからです。

In 1974, I joined the United States Marine Corps. In December of that year, I was sent to a Marine base in Japan. Since I learned Japanese very quickly, and worked in a headquarters office, the United States Communist Party recruited me to be a spy. They disguised themselves as journalists outside the base, where they kept offices.

1974年、私は米海兵隊に入隊しました。その年の12月、日本にある海兵隊の基地に派遣されました。私はすぐ日本語を覚えて、司令部の事務所で働いていましたが、アメリカ共産党は私にスパイになるように働きかけてきました。基地の近くに事務所があり、彼らはジャーナリストを装っていました。

The next day I reported this to my Marine Corps superiors, and became an undercover Naval Intelligence operative. What the Communists were doing was general espionage, helping US troops desert from Japan through Russia to Sweden to escape the Vietnam war, and looking for proof of

162

nuclear weapons on US bases in Japan.

　次の日、私は上官にその経緯を報告し、米海軍情報部局の秘密捜査員になりました。日本にいたアメリカ共産党は、通常のスパイ活動の他に、米兵をロシア経由でスウェーデンに脱走させる手助けをしたり、在日米軍基地に核兵器を持ち込んでいる証拠を探すなどの活動を行っていました。

They also wanted to use the anti-Vietnam war movement in the US, to force America to withdraw US troops from South Korea. Then North Korea would have a chance to attack the South, with no US allies.

　彼らは、米国のベトナム反戦運動を利用して、韓国から米軍を撤退させる活動も行っていました。それが成功すれば、米軍の後ろ盾がなくなった韓国を、北朝鮮が攻撃しやすくなります。

So I can say I fought in the second Korean war. No, it never happened. But there were people who were trying to make it happen. And what I did at that time was dangerous. But I did my duty. And sometimes I experienced first hand secret cooperation between Japan and South Korea in that world of espionage.

　ですので、私は第二次朝鮮戦争を戦っていた、と言えます。まあ、その戦争は現実に起こりませんでしたが、その戦争を起こすために活動している人たちがいたのです。そして、当時の私の任務は危険を伴いましたが、私は自分の義務を果たしました。私は、諜報の世界で日韓が秘密裏に協力しているのをこの目で見てきました。

It was a shadow war, and I am grateful that it never became a real war. But I came to admire Korean people. They are very tough and hard working. I did notice that people were a bit obsessed with proving themselves better than Japan, and always comparing themselves to Japanese people.

Chapter6 The present reality of Japanese/Korean relations

それは影の戦争でした。現実の戦争にならなかったのは嬉しいことです。でも、その時私は韓国人を尊敬しました。とても凛々しく、勤勉でした。自分たちが日本より上であることを証明するために、いつも日本人と比較している姿をよく見ました。

After my time in the Marines, I lived in South Korea for about a year. I noticed that Koreans did not have much contact with other countries. I hoped that such contact would help them to become more sophisticated, and grow out of this obsession with Japan.

私は海兵隊の任期が終わってから、一年くらい韓国に住んでいると、韓国人は他国とはあまり付き合いがないことに気付きました。私は、韓国が外国と関わる機会が増えれば、韓国はもっと常識的な国になり、日本に執着しなくなるのではないかと期待しました。

It was a vain hope. Their obsession with Japan has twisted their National Soul.

残念ながら無理でした。韓国の日本に対する執念は、民族の性質をねじ曲げました。

Korea should learn from Vietnam
韓国はベトナムに学べ

I am not fooled by histrionic Comfort Women performances, sometimes using a wheelchair, sometimes walking. I am not some naive Westerner.

私は、元慰安婦の芝居じみたパフォーマンスに騙されません。私はそんなに鈍感な西洋人ではありません。

All their hysterics about being a WWII victim do not impress me at all. I know the truth. In WWII, Korea was a backwater, there were one or two

164

American air raids on Seoul to my memory. That is all.

　大東亜戦争の犠牲者だというヒステリーは、私に何の影響も与え
ません。私は真実を知っています。大東亜戦争当時、朝鮮は戦争の
直接的影響がほとんどありませんでした。私の調べでは、一回か二
回ぐらい米軍はソウルを空襲しましたが、その程度でした。

　Japan invested much in that country, in 35 years of annexation, Japan
never showed a profit.

　日本は35年の併合時代に、朝鮮に莫大な投資をしましたが、利
益にはなりませんでした。

　And Japan still continues to invest in Korea today. Since the end of the
Korean war, Japan has invested in everything from small scale industries,
hospitals, steel factories, dams, expressways.

　そして今も、日本は韓国に投資を続けています。朝鮮戦争が停戦
すると、日本は小規模工業、病院、製鉄所、ダム、高速道路など、様々
な分野に投資しました。

　How do Korean people show their gratitude? By going around the
world, screaming about how Japan has not properly apologized for
fictional bad deeds supposedly done during the war.

　それに対して、韓国人は日本に感謝の意を表していますか？　日
本が戦争中にひどいことをしたと世界中に嘘を広めて、謝罪しろと
叫んでいるだけではないですか。

　It is not right.

　それは道理に反しています。

　Koreans keep saying that Japan should learn from Germany, that
Germany has truly apologized for what they did in WWII. Well I am of

165

Chapter6 The present reality of Japanese/Korean relations

German aristocratic blood, I know the story well.

　韓国人は、日本に対してよく「ドイツに学びなさい！」と言います。ドイツは第二次世界大戦を心から謝罪している、からだそうです。まあ、私はアメリカ生まれですが、祖先はドイツの貴族なので、ドイツのことはよく分かってます。

But I will tell you, Korean people, you should learn from Vietnam. In the Vietnam war, America devastated that country. America dropped more tonnage of bombs on Vietnam than on both Europe and Asia in WWII. For me, the defoliant weapons dropped were particularly terrible.

　私は韓国人にこう言います。「ベトナムから学びなさい」。ベトナム戦争でアメリカは、第二次世界大戦でヨーロッパとアジアに落とした爆弾より多くの爆弾を、ベトナムに落としました。枯れ葉剤は特に恐ろしくひどいものでした。

South Korea sent a total of some 320,000 troops to Vietnam, and helped devastate that country.

　韓国はアメリカのベトナム焦土化作戦に協力するために、ベトナムにのべ 320,000 人もの兵隊を派遣しました。

I also was a US Marine, so I know that story well.

　私は元米海兵隊ですので、その戦争のことをよく知っています。

But today, the Vietnamese do not cry about being victims. They do not roam all the countries of the world, saying how awful America is. They do not demand money from anybody.

　しかし、今のベトナム人は、自分たちは犠牲者だと叫んだりしません。世界中で、アメリカはひどい国だと言いふらすようなことはしません。他国にお金を要求したりしません。

166

第6章　日韓問題の現実

They are not like Koreans. Whenever Japanese in any outside country meet Koreans in a social situation, the Koreans always scream, "Do you know what Japan did to my country!?!?" Vietnamese people never say to me, since I was born in America, "Do you now what America did to my country?" Even though really most Americans today don't know what America did in Vietnam.

彼らは韓国人と違います。他国の公的な場で日本人と韓国人が一緒になると、韓国人は「日本は私の国に何をしたか知っていますか？」と叫びます。私はアメリカ生まれですが、ベトナム人と会っても、「アメリカが私の国に何をしたか知っていますか？」と言われません。まあ、現在のアメリカ人は、何をしたかほとんど知りませんが。

And their experience is not made up and fictional like the Korean claims are. We could all see it on television.

しかも、ベトナム人の体験は韓国人の言うような作り話ではありません。世界中の人々がテレビでベトナム戦争を見ていました。

What the Vietnamese are doing now is trying to join a trade pact with Japan and America. They look to the future. The past cannot be changed, the Vietnamese are not obsessed with the past. They are a great people.

現在のベトナム人は、日本やアメリカと貿易協定を結ぼうと努力しています。過去は変えられませんから、ベトナム人は過去に囚われず未来に目を向けています。素晴らしい国民です。

In the Pacific War, the Korean people fought as Japanese, as able and willing soldiers under the Emperor. The Korean Crown Prince Yi Un, held the rank of Lieutenant General in the Imperial Japanese Army. He eventually commanded the 1st Air Army which defended the Japanese Home Islands, of the Imperial Army Air force.

167

Chapter6 The present reality of Japanese/Korean relations

　大東亜戦争では、当時の朝鮮人は日本人として、陛下の赤子(せきし)として戦う意志も能力もある兵士でした。李氏朝鮮の李垠(りぎん)皇太子は、日本陸軍の中将にまでなって、日本本土防空の任に当たる第一飛行軍を指揮しました。

It was after the war that Koreans decided they were victims, and roam the world begging someone to punish Japan for them.

戦後になり、韓国人は自分たちは犠牲者であるという話を作り、日本を叩くよう世界中で触れ回っています。

Yi Un, the last Crown Prince of Korea, a Japanese Imperial Army Lieutenant General.

李垠。大韓帝国最後の皇太子。妃は梨本宮守正王第一女子方子。大日本帝国陸軍中将。二・二六事件では鎮圧部隊を直卒。

168

第6章　日韓問題の現実

What the Korean people should do, is learn a lesson from Vietnam.

韓国人がすべきことは、ベトナムから学ぶことです。

Korea's great tragedy was the Korean war, and it was Korean against Korean, not against Japan.

韓国の最大の悲劇は朝鮮戦争でした、日本との戦争ではなく、北朝鮮人と韓国人の戦争でした。

But without Japan, South Korea will wither. It is time to grow up.

日本なしでは、韓国は衰退します。韓国は大人の国になる時です。

169

Chapter 7

Misconceptions
思い違い

A naive peacenik and masochistic view of history
平和ボケと自虐史観

There is a phrase in Japan called "Heiwa Boke". It means a person so befuddled by a peaceful life, that he cannot distinguish reality.

日本語に「平和ボケ」というフレーズがあります。平和な生活で惑わされて、現実が見えないという意味です。

One of the great problems of Japanese society today consists of Article number 9 of the Japanese constitution. There is a custom of regarding written documents as sacrosanct in Asian societies, as something that cannot ever be changed.

現在の日本社会の大きな問題は、憲法第9条です。アジアの国には、書面となった文書は神聖で、侵してはならないという考えがあります。

There is another aspect, that of willingly giving way to others. In Japanese we can call this Enryo suru, or maybe even Jigyaku.

もう一つ問題となるのが、他人に遠慮する、あるいは自虐ということです。

Enryo sure means to give way to, and to give priority to the feelings, wants and needs of others over one's own needs. Jigyaku is more like to self abase oneself, it means something like prostrating yourself before others.

遠慮するというのは、他人が必要とすること、気持ち、要求を、自分が必要とすることより優先することです。自虐の方は、自分を卑下する、他人の前にひれ伏すことです。

There is also a tendency to believe the accusations of other people or authority when someone accuses your own family of wrong doing.

それと、自分の家族が悪いことをしたと訴えられた時、非は身内の方にあると考える傾向があります。

These concepts help to make Japan a wonderful harmonious society to live in. But they are a disaster when dealing with foreigners. And particularly to Americans, living in a self orientated society, these concepts will be nearly incomprehensible.

この概念は、日本での生活においては素晴らしい調和をもたらします。しかし、外国人と付き合う場合には、やっかいな問題を引き起こします。特に、アメリカ人は、自分だけが大切な社会に住んでいるので、こういう概念を理解できないでしょう。

Even today, many Japanese people still do not understand foreign people at all, they assume that foreigners will behave the same way as Japanese people do. No, never.

現在でも、数多くの日本人が、外国人を全く理解していません。外国人も日本人と同じように行動すると考えがちですが、決してそんなことはありません。

Article number 9 is the provision in the Japanese constitution that Japan will never maintain a military and possess the weapons of war.

Chapter7 Misconceptions

第9条は日本国憲法の条項で、日本は永遠に軍隊を持たない、武器を持たないというものです。

Many Japanese people still believe this is the reason that Japan has had peace for the last 71 years. Or they truly believe that America really protects Japan. No.

数多くの日本人は、憲法のおかげで日本は71年間平和が続いてきたと信じています。または、アメリカが実際に日本を守ると心から信じています。違います。

America will only protect Japan if it is in the American interest to do so. There are two reasons for the presence of American military forces in Japan.

アメリカが日本を守るのは、アメリカの国益になる場合だけです。日本にアメリカ軍が存在している理由は二つあります。

One is to prevent Japan from again becoming an independent powerful nation. The other is to send US forces around the world. For American deployments in about half the globe, Japan is the strategic rear.

一つ目の理由は、日本が再び強い独立国にならないようにするためです。二つ目の理由は、米軍を世界中に派遣するためです。日本は地球の半分をカバーするための、重要な後方拠点です。

But America still fears Japan. Well, they fear everybody and everything. So America still keeps a constant barrage of propaganda about how awful Japan was in the Pacific war.

アメリカは今でも日本を恐れています。まあ、彼らは誰にでも、何に対しても、恐れています。それで、アメリカは今もなお、大東亜戦争で日本がいかにひどいことをしたか、というプロパガンダを続けています。

172

第7章　思い違い

The true meaning of article number 9 is that at the end of WWII, Americans looked at Japanese people and saw them as lesser beings, Japanese could not be trusted to have weapons like White Christian nations.

　第9条の本当の意味は、大東亜戦争が終わった時、アメリカ人は日本人が劣位の存在であるべきと考えたということです。アメリカ人は日本人を信用できず、白人キリスト教国のように武装させたくありませんでした。

Considering how many awful and bloody wars White Christian countries conducted, this is very arrogant and condescending thinking.

　白人キリスト教国が行った残虐で、血なまぐさい数多くの戦争を考えると、これはとても傲慢で、見下した考え方です。

And many Japanese continue to believe that Japan was evil in the war.

　しかし、今も大多数の日本人が、日本は戦争で悪いことをしたと信じています。

I have heard all kinds of opinions from people, for example if another country attacked Japan, we should surrender or run away. I have even read about one person who said that we should let an invader kill us all. That way, foreigners would admire Japanese people as a people of peace.

　いろんな人からいろんな意見を聞きました。たとえば、外国が日本を攻撃した場合は、逃げれば良い、あるいは、すぐに降伏すれば良いと言います。またある人は、日本が侵略された場合、抵抗しないで皆殺しにされても良い、と話していました。そうすれば、他国から、日本は平和を愛する国だったと称賛されるということでした。

Really? If Japan was invaded, this person would have gathered his wife and children together and said "Let us go get killed by the invaders,

173

Chapter7 Misconceptions

because we are peaceful." Would his family really accompany him?

　本気なのでしょうか？　日本が侵略された場合、この人物が奥さんと子供たちを集めて、「私たちは平和を愛する国民なので、侵略者に殺してもらいましょう」と言うのでしょうか？　家族は本当に彼についていきますか？

These people are usually of a Leftist political bent, and very kind and nice. But seriously naive and misinformed. And foreigners would not look at Japan in admiration, but they remark how stupid we were for not fighting back.

　こういう人はだいたい政治的には左で、優しい人です。しかし、とても甘い考えで、間違っています。そしてこの場合、外国人は、日本を称賛するのではなく、戦わなかった日本人は愚かだと言います。

Another reason for this Japan was bad propaganda is so that people will not look too closely into American conduct in the war. Of course in war, bad things happen, soldiers kill. But despite what foreigners say, the Imperial Japanese forces were not brutal, and in the main conducted themselves with dignity towards civilians.

　この、日本は悪だったというプロパガンダを行うもう一つの理由は、日本人が、その戦争でのアメリカの行為をしっかり見ないようにするためです。もちろん戦争で悪いことは起こりますし、兵士は人を殺します。しかし、外国人の話でも、日本軍は残虐ではなく、一般人に対して、基本的に威厳ある態度をとっていました。

On the other hand, with such things as strategic bombing, America attempted extinction of the Japanese race. There are still many Americans today who desire this.

　一方、アメリカは戦略爆撃で日本国民の絶滅を試みました。今も、

174

第7章　思い違い

多くのアメリカ人がこれを望んでいます。

And this is what so many Japanese, who cling to the idea that if Japan does not participate in war, does not defend itself, by some miracle war will not happen, do not understand.

それなのに、多くの日本人が、自ら戦うことを放棄すれば、戦争は起きないと思っています。現実を理解していません。

In Chapter 1, I wrote how in Japan's mediaeval wars the common people were not involved. So they do not understand how war is practiced in the rest of the world.

第1章で、日本の戦国時代では民衆は戦争に巻き込まれなかったと書きました。それで、日本人は外国がどんな戦争をやるのか分かっていないのかもしれません。

In the rest of the world, war is about genocide. It is tribe against tribe. It means that my people will kill all of your people, take your land, extinguish your race and culture.

世界の他の国々では、戦争とは、大虐殺です。部族対部族です。自国民が相手国民を皆殺しにして、相手国の領土を奪い、相手国民とその文化を抹殺する、ということです。

And if a country says they love peace and will not fight back, the other country will joyfully massacre you.

もしどこかの国が、我々は平和を愛しているので全く抵抗しません、と言えば、攻撃する国は喜んで皆殺しにします。

By being militarily weak, you invite slaughter by others. It is because Japan was weak after The Pacific war that South Korea landed on Takeshima, Japanese territory. They would not have attempted such a

175

Chapter7 Misconceptions

nation if Japan was strong. They arrested many Japanese fishermen in the area, and some were killed. The fishermen were only released after Japan released Korean criminals from Japanese jails.

　軍事的に弱い国は他国から侵略されます。大東亜戦争後、日本が弱い時に、韓国が竹島に上陸しました。もしその時、日本が軍事的に強い国だったら、韓国はそんなことはしなかったでしょう。竹島の近くで漁をしていた日本の漁船が拿捕され、大勢の漁民が抑留されました。死者も出ています。韓国の要求で、漁師の返還と引き換えに、日本の刑務所から韓国人の犯罪者が大勢釈放されました。

In June of 1953, the Japanese government puts a pillar marking its sovereignty on Takeshima island.

現在韓国に不法占拠されている竹島は、昭和28年6月の時点では行政区域標柱が設置され、日本が管理していた。

第7章　思い違い

Such Japanese people who worship Article number 9 think that Japan was indeed evil, if a war happened again we should immediately surrender. Actually, Japan was lucky at the end the war. One, that America was basically in charge of the occupation. And two, that General Mac Arthur led it.

　第9条を崇拝している日本人は、かつての日本は本当に悪だった、もし戦争が再び起きたらすぐ降伏するべきだと思っています。実際のところ、終戦後の日本は運が良かったのです。その理由の一つ目は、日本を占領したのがアメリカだったことです。二つ目は、マッカーサー将軍がその占領の責任者だったことです。

There were other American officers, that if they had been in charge, would have taken a much more vengeful approach. For example, there were proposals to destroy all Japanese industrial capability, and make Japan an agricultural nation subordinate to America.

　もし他の人物が責任者になっていたら、もっと報復的な行動をとったでしょう。たとえば、日本の産業を完全に潰し、日本をアメリカが支配する農業国にするという話もありました。

America did and still does in the present, attempt to convert Japan culturally into another version of America. But the post war occupation was not as bad as it could have been if another country was in charge.

　昔も、今も、アメリカは日本を小アメリカにするために日本の文化を変革しようとしています。

I have also read comments by some other people, that Japan should surrender if attacked, we should not do something bad to others.

　他国から攻撃された場合、日本は降伏すべきで、他国に悪いことをしてはいけません、というものがありました。

177

Chapter7 Misconceptions

Well, war is indeed evil. But sometimes, to protect your nation and family it is necessary. There is no way to escape this fact. Some people in Japan are incredibly naive on this issue. I have met and talked with such people. They are always very nice and kind. I consider many of them to be friends.

戦争は本当に凶悪です。でも、自分の国と家族を守るために、戦うことが必要な時もあります。この現実を避けることはできません。この問題について、本当に考えが甘すぎる日本人がいます。そういう人と話したことがありますが、本当に優しい人たちです。私の友達にもそういう考えの人がいます。

But they just cannot understand that other countries think differently than Japanese people, and will act differently.

しかし、彼らが理解できないのは、他国の人は日本人とは考えが違うし、行動も違うということです。

There is one more reason for the so called, "peace Constitution". That is that the Japanese military was so powerful, it terrified the Americans. Japan is a very small country, that in a very short time went from nothing to major military and industrial power.

この「平和憲法」なるものが存在するもう一つの理由があります。それは、日本軍が強かったため、アメリカ人が日本を恐れたことです。日本は小さく、狭い国で、何もない所から、短期間のうちに産業的、軍事的に大国になりました。

And on the whole, the Japanese population is more intelligent and certainly more hard working than Americans. Americans do not sleep at night when they think of this, they are terrified. They wish to keep Japan subservient.

基本的にアメリカ人より日本人の方が賢く、一生懸命に働きます。

178

第 7 章　思い違い

アメリカ人がこの事実を考えると、夜も眠れなくなります。日本を怖がっています。だから日本を従属状態にしておきたいのです。

Americans have to let WWII go. They always keep repeating propaganda from that time.

アメリカ人は、大東亜戦争を手放すことが必要です。その当時から、同じプロパガンダを延々と繰り返しています。

Every August, we go through the same media circus ritual. Will a Japanese Cabinet Minister visit Yasukuni shrine? Has Japan properly apologized for the war? American mass media are always bringing this up.

毎年 8 月になると、恒例のメディアのバカ騒ぎがあります。日本の内閣総理大臣は靖国神社を参拝するのか？　日本は過去の戦争をきちんと謝罪しているのか？　アメリカのマスコミは毎年この問題を話題にします。

Well, Americans have not stopped forgiving themselves for their own Civil War of 150 years ago.

まあ、アメリカ人は 150 年前の南北戦争もまだ許していませんが。

But this constant nagging about Japan and the war is beginning to damage the Japanese/ American relationship.

でも、この執拗なあら探しのような日本批判は、徐々に日米関係に傷をつけています。

179

Chapter7 Misconceptions

American misconceptions about the Japanese/Korean governmental agreement
日韓合意とアメリカの思い違い

The recent Japanese/Korean governmental agreement in December of 2015 about the Comfort Women is a case in point.

最近の話では、2015 年 12 月の日韓合意を見るとよく分かります。

American government sources are boasting about success in a government to government agreement that cannot be reversed. This is ridiculous. In a Democracy, any future government has the right to say the actions of previous governments were wrong, hence the change.

アメリカ政府筋は、政府間での不可逆的な合意ができたことを自慢しています。これは愚かなことです。民主主義の場合、将来の政権は、過去の政権が過ちを犯したので、政権交代が起きたのだと言う権利があります。

The US government should not attempt to regulate how other countries view each other's history. America will only make enemies of everybody. I think that the Obama administration feared that the dispute between Japan and Korea would weaken American influence in eastern Asia.

アメリカ政府は、他国間の歴史認識問題に首を突っ込まない方が良いです。このままでは、アメリカは皆の敵になるだけです。私の考えでは、オバマ政権は、この日韓の歴史問題によって、東アジアでのアメリカの影響力が弱まるかもしれないという不安があったのだと思います。

Let me tell you a secret. This agreement has weakened American influence in eastern Asia. There is a lot of anti-American feeling in South

第7章　思い違い

Korea, I have witnessed it. The attack on ambassador Lippert in 2015 was unsuccessful, but Koreans did succeed in killing ambassador Stevens in 1908.

　一つお教えしましょう。この合意により、東アジアでのアメリカの影響力は弱まりました。韓国は反米感情が強いです。私はそれを感じました。2015 年、韓国人はリッパート米大使暗殺に失敗しましたが、1908 年にはスティーブンス大使暗殺に成功しています。

No Japanese has ever killed a US ambassador.

アメリカ大使を殺した日本人はいません。

American Ambassador Stevens and Marquis Itoh, both assassinated by Koreans.

韓国外交顧問ダーハム・ホワイト・スティーブンス（左）と伊藤博文。スティーブンスは 1908 年、サンフランシスコで朝鮮人に射殺された。翌年、伊藤もハルビンで朝鮮人に射殺されている。

Chapter7 Misconceptions

And here is an example of what I meant when I began this chapter. To people outside Japan, since the Japanese government offered an apology for the Comfort Women, it means that Japan was truly evil and awful during the war.

そして、この合意は私がこの章で言いたかったことを示している一つの例です。日本以外の国の人たちは、日本政府が慰安婦問題で謝罪をしたので、日本は本当に戦争の時にひどいことをしていたのだと受け止めたでしょう。

But apologies do not mean that in Japan. In Japanese, it is common to offer an apology even when one did nothing wrong. It gives the other person space, and preserves peace.

しかし、日本では謝罪はそういう意味ではありません。日本では、何も悪いことをしてなくても、謝ることはよくあります。そうすることで、相手の面子を立て、良好な関係を保ちます。

I have seen so many Westerners, particularly Americans, fail to understand this concept, and leave Japan after a few years frustrated and angry. They did not succeed in their venture, because they failed to understand how to communicate as a Japanese.

私が日本に住んでから、数多くの西洋人、特にアメリカ人がこのことを理解できないのを見てきました。彼らは数年で、不満と怒りで日本から出ていきます。彼らが日本での事業に失敗したのは、日本人としてコミュニケーションをとる方法を理解できないからでした。

Of course the Japanese government erred in their understanding of how foreigners would perceive this. What the Japanese government hoped to achieve, and the American government, was an end to the rancor coming from South Korea.

第7章　思い違い

　もちろん、外国人がこの謝罪行為をどう解釈するかということを、日本政府は見誤りました。日本政府、アメリカ政府は、韓国人が日本に対して深い恨みを持つのをやめることを望んでいました。

What both the Japanese and American governments did not understand here is that the South Koreans do not want compensation or money. They see the present existence of Japan as an insult. They wish to force Japanese subjugation to Korea, and have Japan support Korea forever, as a nation ruled and dominated by Korea.

　日本政府やアメリカ政府が分かっていないのは、いくら補償金を渡したところで韓国人は満足しないということです。彼らは日本の存在が許せないのです。彼らが望んでいるのは、韓国が日本を服従させ、日本が韓国の従属国になることなのです。

They cannot let go of that old Confucian thinking, that Korea is superior to Japan because of Confucian scholarship, and geographical proximity to China.

　儒教の考えが根強く、地理的に中国に近い韓国人は、日本人より上位の存在であるという考えを手放すことができません。

This is not going to work out well. In South Korea, when the governmental spokesman announced that Japan would begin to pay money, a riot ensued. And now South Korea groups are demanding more apologies and compensation for other wartime issues, such as ethnic Koreans who were brought to Japan to work in industry.

　日韓合意で問題が続きます。韓国で、政府の報道官がこれから慰安婦問題で日本がお金を支払うことを発表したら、暴動が起きました。それから、韓国の団体が他の戦時の問題、たとえば朝鮮人が日本で強制労働させられた等、新たな謝罪と賠償を要求し始めました。

All Japanese were mobilized to work in the war, and Koreans were

183

Chapter7 Misconceptions

Japanese at the time. Again, if the labor draft had been so arduous, why did it not spark armed revolt in Korea? At that time, there was no significant Japanese military garrison in Korea, and the majority of the police were ethnic Koreans.

　大東亜戦争で日本国民は皆が労働のために動員されましたが、当時朝鮮人も日本国民でした。もしこの動員がひどいものであれば、どうして当時の朝鮮人は武器を持って、暴動を起こさなかったのでしょうか？　朝鮮半島の日本陸軍の守備隊はわずかでしたし、警察官の大多数は朝鮮人でした。

With this anti Japanese hatred that the South Korean government has stoked over the years, they have created a monster that they cannot control. The reason that they let it get so out of hand was to distract people form mistakes by the South Korean government.

　長年にわたって、韓国政府がこの反日感情の火を煽り続けたことで、制御不能の怪物を育て上げてしまいました。怪物がこれほど大きくなってしまった原因は、韓国政府がその失政から韓国人の目をそらすために、反日を利用し過ぎたことでした。

But I think they are now afraid of what they have created.

　しかし、韓国政府にとって、今や自分が育てたこの怪物が恐ろしい存在になってしまいました。

In Japan, this recent Comfort Women agreement has created resentment, and that the overwhelming number of Japanese people. On this issue, the Japanese Left and the Japanese Right are on the same page.

　日本では、この慰安婦問題の合意は圧倒的多数の人が憤慨しています。この問題に関しては、日本の右も左も同じ意見です。

And there is growing resentment at the role of America here. Of course

184

for certain I do not know how much pressure America applied, or in what manner.

　それから、この問題での、アメリカの役割に対しても大きな憤りがあります。もちろん、アメリカがどんな外圧をかけたのかは、私には分かりません。

But I do read certain things written by some influential Americans, and on occasion, I have met influential Americans.

　しかし、私は影響力があるアメリカ人の書いたものをよく読みますし、影響力の強いアメリカ人と会うこともあります。

I am very sorry, but I have never read comments by a powerful American that show that they really understand Japan. Very few speak Japanese, and they only associate with Japanese who deal with foreigners.

　残念ながら、私はそんなアメリカ人の意見で、本当に日本を理解しているなと思えるものを読んだことがありません。日本語ができる人はとても少なく、外国人と関わるのが専門の日本人としか会わないのです。

They do not associate with "The man on the street". The thing is, for example, many business people who deal with foreigners, say things to please foreigners, they may not necessarily say how things truly are. You have to go find that yourself.

　普通の日本人と付き合うことはありません。問題は、外国人と関わるのが専門の日本人、たとえばビジネスマンなら相手の外国人を喜ばせることを言って、真実を言わないのかもしれません。自分でその真実を見いだす必要があります。

And by this action, this Comfort Women agreement, we can see that Americans do not understand the true reasons for the problems between

Chapter7 Misconceptions

Japan and South Korea.

　この慰安婦合意によって、アメリカ人は日韓問題の本当の理由を分かっていないということがよく見えてきます。

It was a serious mistake for America to attempt to regulate historical issues between Japan and South Korea. Japanese are disappointed in America.

　アメリカが日韓の間の歴史問題に関わるのは大きな間違いです。日本人はアメリカに失望しています。

Blindfolded Americans
目隠しをしているアメリカ人

Also, Americans have to let the historical anger go. Pearl Harbor day always being celebrated in America is beginning to rankle in Japan. Frankly, even when I was a child in America, I could not get angry about the Pearl Harbor attack. OK, the Japanese Navy attacked the American Navy, there was a hard war, eventually America won. So what?

　それから、アメリカ人は歴史問題で怒ることをやめなければなりません。真珠湾攻撃の日に特別な儀式を行い続けていますが、それが日本人をいらつかせ始めています。正直に言うと、私はアメリカに住んでいた子供の時も、真珠湾攻撃に対して怒りはありませんでした。日本海軍がアメリカ海軍を攻撃し、激戦が続き、数年後にアメリカが勝った、それだけの話ではないですか。

But Americans make it some kind of religion, that Japan did some great wrong by attacking them. Well we have the American concept of exceptionalism here. Americans think they are the most perfect nation, and that can do no wrong.

第7章 思い違い

しかし、アメリカ人はそれを、ある種の信仰にしています。悪の日本が正義のアメリカを騙し討ちした、という信仰です。これはアメリカ例外主義の考え方です。アメリカ人は、自分たちが世界で最も優れた理想の国であると信じています。自分の国は悪いことはしないと信じています。

I remember in 2003 President Bush started an invasion and bombardment of Iraq with no declaration of war. So why do Americans still, 75 years after the Pearl Harbor attack, call it a sneak attack? Why do they not call their 2003 invasion of Iraq a sneak attack? Why still demonize Japan?

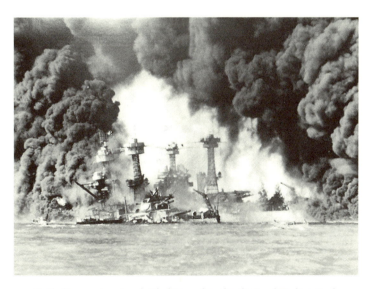

Battleship row, American battleships on fire after the Pearl Harbor attack.

日本機動部隊の攻撃を受け、炎上する真珠湾の米戦艦群。

187

Chapter7 Misconceptions

2003年にブッシュ大統領が宣戦布告をしないでイラクを空襲、侵略を開始しました。それなのに、なぜ、真珠湾攻撃から75年も経っているのに、今も騙し討ちと言うのでしょうか？　なぜ自分たちのイラクへの侵略も騙し討ちと呼ばないのでしょうか？　なぜ日本だけを悪者扱いするのでしょうか？

Americans wear blinders, they cannot imagine doing any wrong. Always the other country is wrong. Concerning Japan, they cling to the propaganda that after The Pacific war, America recreated evil Japan as a good nation.

アメリカ人は視野が狭くて、アメリカが間違ったこと、悪いことをしているということが想像できません。いつも、相手の国が悪いと考えます。大東亜戦争後、アメリカが悪の日本を良い国に作り直したというプロパガンダにしがみついています。

But America has to stop thinking like this, it is causing resentment in Japan.

しかし、アメリカはこんな考え方はやめた方が良いでしょう、日本では反感を買っています。

And with the History issue, too many Americans make judgement on pre-war Japan based on social concepts in the United States today. The Comfort Women issue is a serious example. Many Americans assume that any kind of prostitution is a form of slavery.

歴史問題では、戦前の日本について、現在のアメリカ社会を価値基準にして判断しているアメリカ人が多過ぎます。慰安婦問題は深刻な事例です。多くのアメリカ人は、どんな状況下での売春も性奴隷だと見なします。

But Asians look at it in a much different way. In any case, it is not correct for the American government to be used by some Americans to

188

punish Japan for what it was 70 years ago, but no longer is.

しかし、アジア人の考え方はまるで違います。とにかく、一部の
アメリカ人が、米政府を利用して70年前のことで日本を罰しよう
とするのは、正しいことではありません。

If you want to combat prostitution, why not do something about those
thousands of Korean girls trafficked into the US every year?

もしアメリカ人が売春問題を何とかしたいのなら、どうして現在、
人身売買されてアメリカにいる何千人もの韓国人女性のために活動
しないのですか？

The enduring hatred of the American Civil War
いまだにくすぶる南北戦争

I have my doubts if Americans can put aside history. Even now,
Americans are still fighting about what happened in the American Civil
War of 1861 to 1865.

私は、アメリカ人が歴史に固執するのをやめることができるのか、
疑いを持ってます。現在でも、アメリカ人は1861年から1865年
の南北戦争のことで争っています。

In 2015 there was a big outcry over the use of Confederate symbols
in the US. For example, some State flags in the South still had the
Confederate battle flag, the Stars and Bars, included in their design.

2015年にアメリカで、旧南部連合国のシンボルの使用について
大論争がありました。たとえば、アメリカのいくつかの南部の州が
まだアメリカ連合国の国旗「スターズ・アンド・バーズ」を、その
州旗のデザインに含んでいました。

Chapter7 Misconceptions

Many people in the North cried out that this was prejudice, and it meant that the South was unrepentant.

これに対し、北部の数多くのアメリカ人は、これは南部が戦争を反省していないことを示しており、黒人差別意識の現れであると訴えたのです。

So that is the reason that Americans today criticize Japan about Comfort Women and Yasukuni shrine and Pearl Harbor. If they cannot forgive other Americans, and worry about another war over issues of 150 years ago, how can they ever forget Japan and a war of 70 years ago?

これは、現在のアメリカ人が靖国神社、真珠湾攻撃、慰安婦問題で日本を批判をしているのと同じ理由です。150 年前に戦争をした南部アメリカ人を許せず、またアメリカ人同士の戦争の心配をしているのに、70 年前の日本人との戦争を忘れることができるでしょうか？

And virtually no Americans understand the true causes of the American Civil War. Just as Americans today do not understand that America provoked the attack on Pearl Harbor.

そして、南北戦争の本当の原因を分かっているアメリカ人はほとんどいません。同じように、アメリカが日本を真珠湾攻撃に追い込んだという事実も知りません。

For those Japanese people who think unarmed Pacifism is a good thing, let us take a quick look at the American Civil War. The South and North were very different in culture, and many problems, including the issue of slavery, led the South to declare independence and secede from the Union.

非武装の平和主義が良いことだと考えている日本人のために、ちょっと南北戦争のことをお話ししましょう。当時のアメリカは南部と北部でまるで文化が違い、様々な問題がありました。奴隷制も

190

第7章　思い違い

その中の一つでした。そんな様々な軋轢が原因で南部がアメリカ合衆国から脱退し、アメリカ連合国として独立しました。

The Union could not abide this, mobilized an army and attacked the South. The South simply wanted to be left alone.

北部はこのことを許せず、南部を攻撃しました。南部はただ独立して北部と関わりを持たないことを望んでいただけでした。

Today, Northerners think the war was a humanitarian effort to free slaves, but that is not true. At the time, most Northerners had no desire to free the slaves. It was not until two years into the war that President Lincoln declared all slaves to free, after he was sure he could win the war.

現在の北部のアメリカ人は、南北戦争は奴隷を解放した人道的な活動だと思っていますが、違います。当時、北部に住んでいるほとんどのアメリカ人は、そんなことは考えていませんでした。戦争が始まって2年経ち、北部の勝利が確実になった後、リンカーン大統領は奴隷解放宣言を行ったのです。

There were some 620,000 military deaths in the Civil War, that is not counting civilians. When the North decided to force war and not negotiate, the choices for the South were either surrender and suffer destruction of their society, or fight and try and preserve their society. This is the same type of choice Japan faced from American just before launching The Pacific War.

南北戦争では、620,000人の兵士が死亡しました。この数に、一般人の死亡者は含まれていません。北部が交渉を拒否して、強引に戦争を開始した時に、南部の選択肢は二つでした。降伏して、自分たちの社会と文化の崩壊を受け入れるか、それとも自分たちの社会と文化を守るために戦うか、でした。大東亜戦争開始直前、日本はアメリカの圧力によって、これと同じような選択に迫られたのでした。

191

Chapter7 Misconceptions

In one campaign, Sherman's March to the Sea, he killed 3% of the people who died in that war. This was after the battle of Atlanta, in 1864. Japanese people know this battle from the movie "Gone with the Wind".

著名な作戦の一つに、シャーマン将軍の「海への進軍」があります。彼は南北戦争の全死亡者数の3%を殺しました。これは、1864年のアトランタの戦いの後に起きました。アトランタの戦いを「風と共に去りぬ」の映画で知ってる日本人も多いでしょう。

After that battle General Sherman marched south to the Atlantic coast at the city of Savannah. His army marched in a group 60 miles wide. They destroyed every town and farm they passed through. It was 5 weeks of destruction without one battle.

General Sherman's March to the Sea in the American Civil War, needless destruction, just like the bombing of Japan.

シャーマン将軍の「海への進軍」。鉄道などの基盤、産業施設、個人の資産に至るまで徹底的に破壊し尽くすこの戦略は、後の日本本土空襲と同質のものであった。

第7章　思い違い

　その戦いの後、シャーマン将軍の軍は大西洋岸南部のサバンナまで進みました。シャーマン軍の進軍の幅は 100 キロメートルで、行軍中に軍が通過した街、農家など破壊の限りを尽くしました。戦闘は一度もないまま、5 週間破壊を続けました。

North Korea, a master of deceit
欺瞞の国・北朝鮮

It is not my intention here to say that Americans are exceptionally cruel and bloody. But that is the nature of war. It was to prevent this from happening in Japan that Japanese leaders fought valiantly from the Meiji era until Showa.

　私は、アメリカ人が特に残酷で残忍な国民であると言いたいのではありません。しかし、戦争とはそういうものです。日本はそんな目に遭わないように、明治維新から昭和まで日本の指導者たちが勇敢に戦いました。

And one thing I will say to Americans about this Japan/Korea problem. North Korea is not a military threat. They cannot invade the South, Their missiles always crash. In any case, they do not have much nuclear material. And as the South Koreans lie about the annexation era with Japan, so do the North Koreas lie.

　日韓問題について、アメリカ人に言いたいことが一つあります。北朝鮮に軍事的な危険性はありません。彼らが韓国を侵略するのは不可能です。ミサイルはいつも墜落します。いずれにしても、核物質はあまりありません。韓国人が日本の併合時代について嘘を言うのと同じように、北朝鮮人も嘘を言います。

They exaggerate their military capability. Frankly, I do not believe they

193

Chapter7 Misconceptions

have a working nuclear weapon, I think their nuclear tests are simply masses of conventional explosives laced with nuclear material.

彼らは軍事力を誇張しています。率直に言うと、私は彼らが使える核兵器を持っているとは思いません。核実験は核物質を加えた通常の爆発物を大量に使用したのでしょう。

In an case, even if everything was wonderful for them, the best they could have is only a few nuclear weapons. America has 5,000 nuclear weapons.

仮に実験が上手くいき、本当に核兵器を製造できたとしても、せいぜい4～6個くらいしか造ることはできないでしょう。アメリカは5,000個の核兵器を保有しています。

To start a war with nuclear weapons would be suicide for North Korea. They are not suicidal, even though their actions are often bizarre, they are trying to show the world they are dangerous. They believe they are in danger of attack from America. They make these threats to preserve their nation.

北朝鮮が核戦争を始めるのは自殺行為です。彼らはいつもおかしな行動をとっていますが、自殺的なことはやりません。世界の国々に自分たちが危険な存在であると見せたいだけです。アメリカから攻撃される危険性があると信じているので、自国を守るためにそのように威圧しているのです。

When Madeline Albright visited North Korea as the American Secretary of State, the entire city of Pyongyang was mobilized. All military personnel, governmental workers played parts in a massive theatrical show.

マデレーン・オルブライトはアメリカ国務長官の時に、北朝鮮を訪問しました。その時、平壌市民に動員がかけられました。軍人、

194

第 7 章　思い違い

役人全員が、大がかりな芝居の役者を演じました。

Some people were taxi drivers, some were street vendors of fried meats, some were lined up as passengers for the bus. The streets and stores were filled with busy people, the shelves of the stores visible to the Secretary's motorcade were laden with goods.

タクシー運転手、焼肉の屋台、行列してバスを待つ人などがいました。道も店も人がいっぱいで活気にあふれ、国務長官たちの車列から見える店の棚には商品がたくさん積まれていました。

All this happened on the route Secretary Albright traveled. A few blocks to either side, the streets were deserted as normal. It was all a massive show of deception.

そのルートの両側数ブロック先は、いつもの寂れた通りでした。オルブライトの進行するルートで見られた景色は、全てが大がかりな欺瞞だったのです。

The Korean people, both North and South have this talent for deception, but not for producing real accomplishments. Well, if you look back to the Yi dynasty Korea, before the Japanese annexation, the Yanban class dictated their own reality, nobody could contradict them. It seems that Koreans cannot throw off the burdens of their history.

コリアの国民は、南北ともこのような欺瞞の才能がありますが、欺瞞では、本当の成果を生むことは難しいです。まあ、朝鮮併合時代の前の李氏朝鮮時代を考えると、両班たちは自分たちの好きなように現実を動かし、両班に逆らうグループはいませんでした。やはり、コリアの国民はこの歴史の足かせを外すことはできないようです。

So why worry about a military pipsqueak like North Korea? For America strategically South Korean bases only have meaning in a war against North Korea. They are useless for projecting US power anywhere

195

Chapter7 Misconceptions

else.

　なぜアメリカは北朝鮮のような軍事的に取るに足らない国を、そんなに心配するのでしょう？　アメリカにとって、戦略的に韓国にある軍事基地は北朝鮮との戦争にしか使えません。地球の他の地域を支援するための戦力拠点としては役に立たないでしょう。

What America should strive for
アメリカが目指すべきもの

But Japan is strategically vital for the US. Without the bases in Japan, America cannot fight in the Middle East, or anywhere in Asia.

　しかし、アメリカにとって、日本は戦略的に必要不可欠です。日本の基地がなければ、アメリカはアジアや中東で戦争ができません。

I do not agree with most American wars, but this is fact.

　私はアメリカの戦争にはほとんど賛成していませんが、これは事実です。

Also, Japanese people, genuinely like Americans. I can say that all Japanese people of all political persuasions do. Some may not like certain American policies, but they like American people and culture.

　また、日本人は、実にアメリカ人のことが好きです。どんな政治信条の人もアメリカ人が好きです。アメリカの政策が嫌いな人はいますが、それでもアメリカ人やアメリカの文化は好きです。

This was also true in 1941. America provoked Japan into attacking the US in the mistaken belief that it was China that would be America's servant in Asia.

196

第7章 思い違い

1941年の真実はこうでした。アメリカは中国がアジアでの自国の僕であるという間違った認識に立ち、日本がアメリカを攻撃するよう追い詰めました。

That was a total mistake. If America had made a partnership with Japan then, the world would be a much better place today.

これは完全な間違いでした。当時、アメリカが日本と協力的な関係を作っていたら、今の世界はもっと良い世界になっていたでしょう。

Americans should stop worrying about whether Japan will become a military state again, should look at how to strengthen our partnership for the future.

アメリカ人はもう、日本が再び軍事国家になるんじゃないかと心配するのはやめて、将来のために日本との協力関係をいかに強化するか考えるべきです。

The fantasy of reunification
南北統一の幻想

As for the Koreans, they are way too emotional for their own good.

韓国人についてですが、彼らは自分たちの利益のために感情的になり過ぎです。

What do I mean?

私が言いたいのはこういうことです。

One of the true intents of South Korean groups who keep up all this trouble about history is to join North and South Korea together, and then

Chapter7 Misconceptions

attack, destroy, and humiliate Japan.

日本との歴史問題で騒いでいる韓国の団体の本当の目的は、北朝鮮と韓国を統一することと、日本を攻撃して、その信用を失墜させ、恥をかかせることです。

In their minds, they will then have created the greatest nation on earth.

そうすれば世界で最も素晴らしい国が創れると考えているようです。

There are many problems and dangers with this thinking.

この考え方には、たくさんの問題と危険性があります。

One, these Southern groups are in a real hurry for reunification. Now, I am an ethnic German, and I know something about this. I watched the reunification of East and West Germany with great interest.

一つは、統一を願う韓国の団体はとにかく早く統一したいと考えています。まあ、私はドイツ人なので、このことについては多少分かります。私は東西ドイツの統一を注視していました。

First of all East Germany was the showplace of the Communist world. Yet only 10% of households had a telephone. The cultural and economic gap with West Germany was huge.

まず、東ドイツは共産主義世界における模範国家でした。それでも電話がある家は10％程度しかありませんでした。東と西ドイツの文化的なギャップはとても大きいものでした。

After unification, 80% of East Germans had to find a new profession. Some of the East German military enlisted personnel and equipment, notably Mig-29 fighters were kept. But all East German military officers had to quit.

統一後、80％の元東ドイツ人は職業を探す必要がありました。

第 7 章　思い違い

東ドイツ軍の一部の下士官兵と装備、たとえばミグ 29 戦闘機はドイツ軍に残りましたが、将校は全員除隊させられました。

After reunification, politically, socially, economically, the West totally dominated the East.

統一後、政治的にも、社会的にも、経済的にも西が東を支配しました。

Today, the Eastern part of Germany still lags behind the West economically, and Western prejudice toward Easterners still exists.

現在もドイツの東側は経済的に遅れていて、西ドイツ人による東ドイツ人に対する差別が今もあります。

But there was contact between the two Germanys in the cold war. They could send mail to each other. Phone calls could be made. West Germans could freely enter East Germany. Once East Germans reached retirement age, they could go West.

しかし、冷戦時代も東西ドイツの間で、ある程度関係が保たれていました。お互いに郵便を送ることができましたし、電話をかけることもできました。西ドイツ人は自由に東ドイツに入国することができましたし、東ドイツ人は定年したら、西ドイツに入ることもできました。

North and South Korea on the other hand, have had virtually no contact. The only way for a North Korean to go to South is an arduous journey through China at the risk of their lives.

それに対して、北朝鮮と韓国の間では、そんなことはほとんどありません。北朝鮮人が南へ行くには、中国を経由して命がけで困難な旅をするしか方法がありません。

199

Chapter7 Misconceptions

In the years since the Korean war, the language of both nations has grown apart, some 30% of each language is now unintelligible to the other.

朝鮮戦争後、次第に南北の言葉が変化したため、現在、お互いに3割程度の言葉を理解できません。

In 1904 when the Russo/Japanese war started, Koreans only had to worry about Japan and Russia.

1904年の日露戦争開戦時、李氏朝鮮が懸念すべきは日本とロシアだけでした。

But now China is also a great power, and America lurks behind Japan, reunification is so much more complicated, and Koreans are too unrealistic and emotional.

しかし今は、中国も大国になり、日本の背後にはアメリカも控えています。統一は本当に複雑で困難になっているのに、今の韓国人は現実的ではなく、感情的になり過ぎです。

A quick reunification will definitely result in Civil War. North Korea is isolated, but I think some things are easy to understand. When Nicolae Ceasescu, President of Romania and his wife were executed in 1989 Kim Jong Il of North Korea showed films of the event to elite North Koreans.

急な統一では絶対に内乱になります。北朝鮮は孤立している国ですが、解りやすい側面もあると思います。ルーマニアのニコラエ・チャウシェスク大統領が1989年に処刑された時、北朝鮮の金正日は自国のエリートたちにその処刑の映像を見せました。

He said that if they did not hold together, this would happen to them. And he was right. If we look at the unification of Germany, the prosperous West completely dominated the East.

彼のメッセージは、北朝鮮のエリートも団結して努力しないと、こ

第7章　思い違い

のように処刑されるぞ、ということです。彼は正しかったです。ドイツの統一では、繁栄している西側が東側を完全に飲み込みました。

The gap between North and South Korea is extreme. Something like this would be bound to happen in rushed unification. The Northerners would attempt to dominate the South using the same Southern people who demonstrate about the Comfort Women and other anti Japan issues.

　北朝鮮と韓国の間にあるギャップはとても深いです。急な統一では、東西ドイツの統一のようなことが起きてしまいます。北朝鮮人は、慰安婦問題などで反日活動をやっている韓国人たちを使って、韓国に影響を及ぼし、優位に立とうとするでしょう。

They would hold up a dream of a united strong Korea. But they would be desperate. It would ignite a Civil War. Russia, China, Japan, and the US would all interfere, all of us would wonder, what kind of Korea will arise from this mess? Let us try to ensure that it will be a Korea that reflects our interests.

　韓国人たちは強い統一コリアという夢を抱いています。しかし、それは無謀です。その結果、内乱になれば、ロシア、中国、日本、アメリカが介入してきます。この四ヵ国は、今後コリアがどういう国になるのかを考え、コリアが自分たちの国益にかなう国になるように働きかけるでしょう。

This is exactly what happened when the last of the Yi dynasty could not make up their mind whether to look to Russia or Japan, they thought they could play some sort of balancing game.

　李氏朝鮮時代の末期も同様のことが起きました。彼らはロシアにつくか、日本につくかを決められなかったのです。日露両国の間で、何とか均衡を保ったまま存在できると思ったのかもしれません。

They had no comprehension of the outside world, and because of

201

Chapter7 Misconceptions

centuries of intrigue and incompetent domestic rule, no competent officials to manage the country's affairs.

彼らは自分の国の外で起きていることを、全く理解していませんでした。それに、何世紀も続いた無能な支配と策謀で、国を運営できるような有能な人材が育っていませんでした。

The result was annexation by Japan. In this age, I do not think that will repeat itself. In the Korean war of 1950 to 1953, world nuclear war was avoided by the Russians and Americans agreeing to restore the status quo, a front line near the 38th parallel.

その結果、日本に併合されたのです。今の時代、それは繰り返されないでしょう。朝鮮戦争の時は、戦争前に米ソが取り決めた 38 度線付近に軍事境界線を引くことで合意し、核戦争は回避されました。

But in a modern civil war Korea would be devastated. Many would die. There would be risk of world wide nuclear war. I understand the desire for reunification. But you cannot be emotional.

しかし今、内乱が起こって現代の兵器が使用されれば、コリアは崩壊するでしょう。数多くの人が亡くなるでしょうし、世界的な核戦争に発展する可能性もあります。統一したいという気持ちは分かりますが、感情だけで動いてはダメです。

Even if you do succeed in reunifying, it will result in the movement of people. And it will be from North to South. Infrastructure is non existent in the North, they don't have electricity 24 hours a day.

統一が成功しても、人間が移動するだけの結果となります。北から南への移動のみです。北朝鮮にはインフラはありません。1 日 24 時間使える電気は流れていません。

202

第 7 章　思い違い

Not many Southerners will want to live there. Life would be too primitive. Yet the Northerners who come to the South, would not comprehend what a Capitalist society is, they would not be able to compete on normal terms.

　北の生活は原始的過ぎて、そこに住みたいと思う南の人はほとんどいないでしょう。しかし、南へ行く北の人々は資本主義社会を理解していないので、現代の競争社会に容易に適応できません。

Since in this scenario, some sort of collapse of authority would happen in the North, they would be well armed. There are all sorts of arms depots for reserve forces scattered across North Korea.

　このシナリオでは、北の軍や警察も崩壊しているので、南へ流入する人たちは武装しているでしょう。北朝鮮のあちこちに予備役のための兵器庫があります。

So the Northerners who come South would have weapons. And they have grown up in hardship, and will much tougher than Southerners both physically and mentally.

　それに、苦しい生活の中で育ってきたのですから、南の人より精神的にも肉体的にも強いです。

The result will be an explosion in the number of nasty criminal gangs in South Korea. This is not any kind of derogatory statement about Korean character, this is reality. Things were pretty bleak in Russia when the Soviet Union collapsed.

　その結果、韓国国内で厄介な暴力集団が急増するでしょう。これはコリアンの国民性を侮辱しようというものではなく、現実の話です。ソ連崩壊後のロシアも、とても厳しい状況になりました。

Again, in Korea there will be much social disorder, and many people

203

Chapter7 Misconceptions

will die.

　そして、コリアで起こる社会的混乱、暴動で、数多くの人々が亡くなるでしょう。

Be realistic, it will take decades of hard work on all sides. But you will need truth in education in your own country, South Korea. This anti Japan activity must stop. It has no basis in truth. It is producing Koreans who do not know their true history, they will be unable to function in the world.

　現実的になってください。統一は関係各国の何十年間にもわたる協力を必要とします。しかし、そのためには韓国自身が正しい教育をしなければなりません。一連の反日活動をやめる必要があります。実際、その活動には根拠がありません。反日教育によって、自分たちの本当の歴史を知らない韓国人が大量生産されました。彼らは、世界でまともに機能できないでしょう。

Korea's true tragedy, the Korean War
コリアの本当の悲劇「朝鮮戦争」

And remember, the only country that has ever treated the Korean people with compassion, and regard for their advancement and well being, is Japan. And by constantly funding various projects in Korea, Japan still does.

　それから、これまでにコリアの国民に同情し、その生活向上に尽力した国は日本だけであることを覚えておいてください。今も日本は韓国に対して様々な分野で支援を続けています。

All countries that have had wars have had difficult times. But Japan did nothing evil to you, it is the other way around, Japan made every effort to raise you up to an equal level.

第7章　思い違い

　戦争が経験したどの国も、厳しい時期がありました。しかし、日本は韓国に対してひどいことはしていません。むしろ逆で、日本は韓国を日本と対等なレベルに引き上げる努力をしてきました。

And all this anti Japan education, and world wide anti Japan activity such as building Comfort Women statues can only hurt Koreans.

　反日教育や、世界中に慰安婦像を設置することは、韓国人にとって不利益になります。

When Koreans travel overseas, they learn that much of their education has been a lie. This will devastate people, and when they return to Korea, they are a potential revolutionary group.

　韓国人が海外に旅行すると、自分の受けた教育の多くが嘘だと分かります。これは彼らを困惑させます。そして韓国へ帰る時には反政府的なグループになっている可能性があります。

Here I would like to describe Korea's true tragedy, the Korean War.

　これからコリアの本当の悲劇、朝鮮戦争について説明します。

The Soviet Russian attack into Manchuria began on August 9th, 1945. The Russian tank forces were highly skilled in armored warfare, having defeated Germany. Since Japan had no large tank units of their own, and the best units had been withdrawn from Manchuria to fight America, the Russians quickly penetrated and took major cities.

　ソ連による満洲への攻撃は 1945 年 8 月 9 日に始まりました。ドイツを打ち破ったソ連の機甲師団は、戦車戦に非常に熟練していました。日本軍には強力な戦車部隊がなく、さらに満洲にいた精鋭部隊が対米戦のために満洲から引き抜かれていたので、ソ連部隊は容易に侵入し、満洲の主な都市を占領しました。

205

Chapter7 Misconceptions

Japan surrendered on August 15th, but fighting in Manchuria continued for some time. But in late August, all Japanese forces in Manchuria and northern Korea surrendered to Soviet Russian forces.

日本の降伏は8月15日でしたが、その後しばらくの間満洲での戦いが続きました。しかし、8月の終わりまでに、満洲、朝鮮半島の北部にいた日本軍は全てソ連軍に降伏しました。

On August 18 Soviet forces made amphibious landings in northern Korea. The Russian advance stopped at the 38th parallel as agreed with America.

8月18日ソ連軍が朝鮮半島の北部に侵入しましたが、アメリカとの合意により、ソ連軍の進攻は38度線で止まりました。

US forces landed at Inchon on September 8th 1945. But Japanese military and police units carried on their functions under American orders south of the 38th parallel until enough American units could arrive to establish law and order. But all such Japanese forces were disarmed by the Americans within a few months after the surrender, and returned to Japan.

1945年9月8日、米軍部隊が輸送船で仁川に到着し、上陸を始めました。アメリカの部隊はまだ数が少なかったので、38度線の南側で米軍部隊の数が揃うまで、秩序維持のため日本の軍と警察がアメリカの指示で任務を続けていました。しかし、数ヵ月後、全ての日本軍・警察はアメリカ軍に武装解除されて、日本に帰国しました。

By the end of 1945, there were no Japanese forces whatsoever in the Korean peninsula.

1945年の終わりには、朝鮮半島に日本兵は一人もいなくなりました。

第 7 章 思い違い

Both Soviet Russia and America established a client state on their own sides of the 38th parallel. In the North, the Russians made Kim Il Sung, a former Soviet Army officer, leader, in the South, America chose Rhee Syngmun.

アメリカとソ連は 38 度線の南北にそれぞれ自分の従属国を創りました。北側では元ソ連軍の士官である金日成を指導者として立て、南側ではアメリカは李承晩を選びました。

Kim Il Sung of North Korea, Rhee Syngman of South Korea with General Mac Arthur.

若き日の金日成（上）と李承晩、マッカーサー。

207

Chapter7 Misconceptions

From this time on in the South there was a serious guerrilla insurgency, some 8,000 guerrillas were active. Their areas of operation were in Andong area, the Taebaek, Odae, and Chiri mountain regions.

この時から韓国内で本格的なゲリラによる反乱が始まり、8,000 人のゲリラが戦闘を開始しました。活動の地域は、安東の辺り、太白山地、五台山と智異山でした。

In counter guerrilla operations, President Rhee killed many Koreans, and it was this wave of refugees from this time that accounts for the presence of so many ethnic Koreans in Japan to this day.

ゲリラ討伐の際、李大統領が多くの韓国人を殺したので、この時発生した難民が日本に流れ、その多くが現在の在日韓国・朝鮮人になっています。

The story that there were forced laborers brought to Japan is another Korean falsehood, they were refuges from South Korean repression.

労働者として日本に強制連行されてきたというのは、もう一つの韓国人の嘘です。彼らは韓国から流れてきた難民でした。

In 1950, June 25th, the North Koreans launched a massive offensive. They had a well trained army of over 200,000 men. The core of this army was some 40,000 men who had fought with the Soviet Army in WWII, battle experienced veterans.

1950 年 6 月 25 日に北朝鮮が大規模な攻撃を開始しました。20 万人以上の精鋭兵士がいましたが、その中心は第二次世界大戦でソ連軍と一緒に戦った 4 万人の実戦経験者でした。

The North Koreans also possessed 150 tanks and 130 combat aircraft.

北朝鮮軍は戦車 150 台と戦闘機 130 機も保有していました。

208

第 7 章　思い違い

South Korea did not have one tank, and only a few trainer aircraft. One third of the men did not have a uniform. Many used Japanese rifles from Japanese depots left behind in Korea. South Koreans troops fought bravely, soldiers even tried to destroy North Korean tanks with suicide bombs.

韓国軍には戦車が 1 台もなく、飛行機は練習機が数機あるだけでした。三分の一の韓国兵は軍服がなく、多くの韓国兵は日本軍の倉庫に残っていた武器を使用しました。韓国軍は勇敢に戦い、北朝鮮の戦車を破壊するために、兵士が爆弾を抱えて自爆攻撃しました。

The reason was America simply did not supply enough weaponry. They did not think South Korea to be very important.

アメリカは、韓国をそれほど重要だとは考えておらず、十分に武器を供給していませんでした。

But to no avail.

韓国軍では力不足でした。

The North Koreans quickly advanced into Seoul, and the Korean government fled to Pusan. It was here that arrival of many American units stabilized the line.

北朝鮮軍が一気にソウルを占領して、韓国政府は釜山に逃げました。釜山にアメリカ軍が続々と到着し、戦線を維持しました。

General Mac Arthur counter attacked by an amphibious landing at Inchon, and advanced into North Korea. The North Korean army was basically cut off in the south near Pusan, they took to the mountains to conduct guerrilla warfare. The Chinese Army sent massive amounts of troops into Northern Korea unnoticed by America.

マッカーサー将軍が仁川上陸作戦で反撃を開始して、北朝鮮側に進攻しました。北朝鮮軍の多くは釜山附近に展開していたので、分

209

Chapter7 Misconceptions

断され、山に逃げ込みゲリラ戦を始めました。一方中国は、アメリカの知らぬ間に北朝鮮に大軍を送り込みました。

In a great offensive, the Chinese army drove to a line south of Seoul. The UN command gradually drove the Chinese north to the present Demilitarized line, where fighting continued on that line for two years while negotiations ensued.

中国軍は猛攻撃を開始して、ソウルを越えてさらに南下しましたが、国連軍の反撃を受け、徐々に今の軍事境界線附近まで押し戻され、その線で2年間、膠着した状態が続きました。その間、停戦交渉が続けられました。

United Nations forces in the Korean war.
朝鮮戦争に参戦した国連軍の戦車部隊。

第 7 章　思い違い

America had about 5 Army and one Marine division, Great Britain sent a division, Turkey, sent a brigade, Thailand, Canada, and the Philippines regimental sized forces, France a battalion, many other countries contributed forces, including tiny Luxembourg, which sent 44 men.

アメリカは陸軍 5 個師団と海兵隊の 1 個師団、英国は 1 個師団、トルコは 1 個旅団を派遣しました。タイ、カナダ、フィリピンは連隊クラスの部隊を派遣し、フランスは 1 個大隊でした。数多くの国が兵士を派遣して、ルクセンブルクのような小さい国も 44 人を派遣しました。

A cease fire was concluded in 1953, and the situation stays the same today, but it is still tense, with many incidents happening. When I lived in South Korea in the late 1970's it was common that the North would send commandos into South Korea, by fishing boat, and shoot up some coastal village until they were caught and killed.

1953 年に停戦となってから現在まで同じ状態が続いています。しかし、今も緊張が続いており、多くの事件が起きている状態です。私が韓国に住んでいた 1970 年代には、北朝鮮が漁船で特殊部隊を韓国に送り込み、どこかの漁港に上陸し、自分たちが全滅するまで民間人を殺しまくるという事件がよくありました。

Guerrilla warfare by Communists originally living in South Korea and remnants of the Northern army which invaded the South continued resistance behind the lines until 1955/1956.

最初から韓国にいた共産主義者と、韓国国内に取り残され、潜伏したままの北朝鮮軍は、1955 年、1956 年まで、ゲリラ戦を展開しました。

The last South Korean guerrilla was finally captured in 1963.

韓国にいた最後のゲリラは 1963 年にようやく捕まりました。

211

Chapter7 Misconceptions

One thing here, while during the annexation period, the Japanese government was aware of Communist underground political activity in areas of South Korea, there were no Communist uprisings.

併合時代、朝鮮に共産主義の地下組織があることを日本政府は知っていました。しかし、共産党員によるゲリラ戦はありませんでした。

This is because the Korean people would not support such an underground uprising against Japanese rule. It was the post WWII chaos that the Communists were able to make such revolts.

朝鮮人は当時の日本統治に大きな不満はなく、反乱を支持しなかったからです。大東亜戦争後の混乱で、共産主義ゲリラに反乱のチャンスが訪れたのです。

What Koreans should strive for
韓国人は何を目指すのか？

Also, foreigners are becoming tired of constant Korean complaining. And more and more foreigners are learning the truth of what happened in the war. The truth always comes out eventually. But when foreigners discover the truth about this Japanese / Korean issue, they will see Koreans as a people to be shunned.

それから、外国人は韓国人の止むことのない反日の主張にうんざりしています。外国人も大東亜戦争で何があったのか、少しずつその事実を学んできています。真実はいずれ広まるものです。しかし、外国人がこの日韓問題の真実を知ってしまうと、韓国人は世界中の人々から敬遠されるようになると思います。

Is that your goal?

212

第 7 章　思い違い

　韓国人はそんなことを目指しているのですか？

You must quit blaming Japan for your shortcomings, it has been more than 70 years since the war ended, what stops you from becoming a great country? Look in the mirror.

　韓国人たちは、自分たちの短所を日本のせいにするのをやめるべきです。終戦から 70 年も経っているのに、なぜ大国になれないのでしょうか？　鏡を見てください。

Afterward
おわりに

In Chapter 5, all of the statistics come from the book "The New Korea" written by Alleyne Ireland. It is an excellent book for the scholar of Japanese/Korean annexation period, it is full of facts about just how Japan did to raise Korea up to a comparable level of civilization.

第5章の統計データは全て、アレン・アイルランド著『朝鮮が劇的に豊かになった時代』から引用しました。この本は朝鮮併合時代を学ぶ者にとって素晴らしい情報源であり、日本がどれほど、当時の朝鮮を日本と同じ文化レベルに引き上げようと努力したかについて、数多くの真実が書かれています。

This book, "1907 in Korea with Marquis Ito" provides an excellent description of daily life and the physical condition of Seoul and other cities just before the Japanese annexation.

ジョージ・トランブル・ラッド著『1907 IN KOREA WITH MARQUIS ITO（伊藤侯爵と共に朝鮮にて)』は、朝鮮併合前のソウルや他の街の様子、人々の日常生活が紹介された素晴らしい内容です。

Both books are available in Japan in an English and Japanese language edition.

どちらも、日本で日英二ヵ国語版が出版されています。

As for my statements about Korean falsehoods, may I direct you to this newspaper article. " A low-trust society" The Korea Herald English

おわりに

edition. 2011.8.02. The article states frankly that one of the biggest social problems in Korea is lying. Constant lying.

韓国人の嘘の問題については、次の新聞記事を読んでください。"A low-trust society" The Korea Herald 英語版（2011 年 8 月 2 日）。この記事は、現在の韓国社会の一番の問題は、嘘をつくこと、絶えず嘘をつき続けていることだ、と率直に書いています。

Concerning the slave salt farms that exist in South Korea today, please read The Independent, "The islands of abuse: Inside South Korea's slave farms for the disabled" January 3, 2015.

韓国の塩田での奴隷労働については、英国の新聞インデペンデントの、2015 年 1 月 3 日の記事 "The islands of abuse: Inside South Korea's slave farms for the disabled" を読んでください。

I had my own problems with that aspect of Korea when I lived there. I worked in 3 different Hagwon, or English language school in Korea. They all refused to pay me at the end of the month. The only school that paid me was an American run school. It was this constant problem that caused me to leave Korea and return to Japan.

私が韓国に住んでいたとき、同様の問題を実際に体験しました。私が働いた 3 ヵ所のハグァン（英会話学校）は、月末にギャラを支払ってくれませんでした。ちゃんとギャラを支払ったのは、アメリカ人が経営する学校だけでした。こういうことがよくあったので、私は韓国を去り、日本に戻りました。

I have seen American State Department travel advisories, that one should not believe any Korean person about working conditions in a Korean English school. Only believe another American who has worked there.

アメリカ外務省の渡航者安全情報の注意を読むと、韓国の英会話

学校で仕事をする場合、仕事の条件について韓国人の話を信じては
いけません、と書かれています。信用できるのは、その学校で働い
ているアメリカ人の話だけです。

But I sincerely hope Koreans can outgrow these wild fantasies about the
war, and find a way to cooperate with Japanese people for the future.

私が切に願うのは、韓国人が　被害妄想から脱却し、将来のため
に日本人と互いに協力する道を模索してほしい、ということです。

But I will wait and see.

成り行きを見守ろうと思います。

I sincerely hope that Americans can stop complaining about Japan and
The Pacific War. But since Americans are still arguing about their own
Civil War of 150 yeas ago, I am not optimistic about this.

また私は、アメリカ人は大東亜戦争や当時の日本を批判するの
をやめてほしい、と思っています。しかし、アメリカ人は今も 150
年前の南北戦争について論争しているくらいですから、これに関し
ては悲観的です。

For Japan, as we face an uncertain future of very limited resources, it is
time to recreate the society Japan had in the Edo era, confidence in one's
own country and culture, everybody has a place and function in society.
Things were used and reused. We must stop being attracted by foreign
philosophies, such as the American idea that a huge wealth gap is a good
idea.

世界は資源が乏しくなる暗い将来に向かっています。日本は江戸
時代のような社会を取り戻すべきです。江戸時代、人々は自分たち
の文化に自信を持ち、社会の中でそれぞれの立場で機能していまし
た。物が再利用され、「もったいない」という哲学が大切にされて

おわりに

いました。外国の哲学、たとえば、格差があるのは当たり前で良いことだ、というアメリカ人みたいな考えはやめるべきです。

America is tipping into Civil War. Instead, Japan should lead the world by example, and show other countries how to prosper in these difficult times ahead.

アメリカは現在内乱へと向かっています。これから迎える前途多難の時代をどう乗り越えるか、日本は他国の手本となって世界を導かなければなりません。

And my thanks to many more people I have no space to mention here, who helped make this book possible.

この本は、ここに書き切れないほどたくさんの方々の協力があり、出版することができました。心から感謝しています。

マックス・フォン・シュラー

Notice

Notice
注記

※以下、本文中で使用される用語についての説明です。

◆「李氏朝鮮」は朝鮮併合以前の朝鮮半島を意味します（大韓帝国も含みます）。

◆「朝鮮」、「当時の朝鮮」は朝鮮併合時代の朝鮮半島を意味します。

◆「北朝鮮」、「韓国」は現在の朝鮮半島の二つの国を意味します。

◆「コリア」、「コリアン」は南北両国家国民、あるいは将来統一された後の国家国民を意味します。

Book List
参考文献

The New Korea

著者：Alleyne Ireland
出版：E. P. Dutton Japanese translation Sakuranohana
邦題：朝鮮が劇的に豊かになった時代
日英対訳：桜の花出版（2013）

　This work is a must for anyone studying the Japanese/Korean relationship. It provides an extremely detailed scholarly account of Japanese development of Korea.

　この本は日韓問題の研究のためには絶対必要です。詳細かつ学術的に日本の朝鮮併合時代の朝鮮開発を説明しています。

In Korea with Marquis Ito

著者：George Trumball Ladd
出版：Longmans, Green & Co.
邦題：1907　伊藤侯爵と共に朝鮮にて
日英対訳：桜の花出版（2015）

　Mr. Ladd spent several months in Korea on the eve of annexation, and gives an interesting account of Korean society and life at that time.

　ラッド氏は併合直前に数ヵ月朝鮮を旅しました。彼の当時の朝鮮の社会と生活の話はとても面白いです。

Getting Over It!

著者：Sonfa Oh（呉善花）
出版：Tachibana Publishing
邦題：なぜ「反日韓国に未来はない」のか
出版：小学館新書（2013）

A very good description of how anti-Japanese education was promoted in the post war years, how the anti Japanese relationship evolved in Korea, and the dangers for Korea in the future of this course.

戦後の韓国における反日教育の推進を説明することで、韓国人の反日思想がどのように進化していったかを解説しています。この状況がなぜ韓国の未来にとって危険であるか、はっきりと警鐘を鳴らしています。

America encounters Japan

著者 :William Louis Neumann
出版 :Torchbooks
邦題：アメリカと日本—ペリーからマッカーサーまで
出版：研究社出版（1986）

A very good account of the pre-war years. It details the efforts of Christian missionaries to aid China and Christianize it, panic about Japan from Californians, and the efforts of the FDR administration to force Japan into starting war.

戦前について書いている良い本です。中国を日本から救うアメリカのキリスト教宣教師団のこと、カリフォルニアに日本軍が攻めてきたと全米がパニックに陥ったこと、フランクリン・D・ルーズベルト政権が日本を戦争に追い込んだことについて詳しく書かれています。

Soldiers of the Sun: The rise and fall of the Imperial Japanese Army

参考文献

著者 :Meirion Harries
出版 :Random House

A history of the Japanese Imperial Army. The notation of only 17 military police at Nanking is on page 230.

日本軍の歴史について書かれた本です。特筆すべきポイントとして、南京事件当時、南京には憲兵が 17 人しかいなかったということが 230 ページに書かれています。

Day of Deceit The truth about FDR and Pearl Harbor

著者 :Robert Stinnett
出版 :Touchstone
邦題：真珠湾の真実 — ルーズベルト欺瞞の日々
出版：文藝春秋（2001）

The FDR administration's 8 point plan to force Japan into starting war is on page 8. The book details how the FDR administration knew the attack on Pearl Harbor was coming.

フランクリン・D・ルーズベルト政権が日本を戦争に追い込んだ 8 つの計画を 8 ページに書いています。この本は、ルーズベルト政権が戦争が始まる前から真珠湾攻撃を知っていたことについて説明しています。

Embracing Defeat: Japan in the wake of WWII

著者 :John W. Dower
出版 :Norton
邦題：敗北を抱きしめて―第二次大戦後の日本人（上・下）
出版：岩波書店（2004）

Explains how the Tokyo War Crimes trials were extremely unfair, totally unjust.

東京裁判がいかに不公平で不公正なものだったのかを説明している本です。

221

Book List

War without Mercy: Pacific War

著者 :John W. Dower
出版 :PANTEON BOOKS
邦題：容赦なき戦争─太平洋戦争における人種差別
出版：平凡社（2001）

Describes the propaganda efforts of Japan and the US in the war. Also mentions how US troops killed 50% of surrendering Japanese troops.

戦争中の日本とアメリカのプロパガンダについて説明しています。また、日本兵が米軍に投降した場合、その半数が殺害されたことが書かれています。

What Soldiers Do: Sex and the American GI in France

著者 :Mary Louise Roberts
出版 :Chicago
邦題：兵士とセックス─第二次世界大戦下のフランスで米兵は何をしたのか？
出版：明石書店（2015）

Describes how American troops raped, pillaged and forcefully bought women for sex across France in WWII. Also mentions the American Comfort Women system in Hawaii in WWII.

第二次世界大戦でアメリカ兵がフランスの至る所で強盗し、女性をレイプし、強制的に売春させていたことを説明しています。そして、アメリカのハワイの慰安婦システムについても書かれています。

This Kind of War

著者 :T. R. Fehrenbach
出版 :Macmillian

Describes the lack of morale and fighting ability of the US 2nd infantry division in the Korean war, when faced with difficulty. Also describes the collapse of American society among US POW's in Korea.

朝鮮戦争での米第2歩兵師団の士気低下と戦力について分析しています。そして、朝鮮における米兵捕虜の社会崩壊について説明しています。

A Republic, Not an Empire: Reclaiming America's Destiny

著者 :Patrick J. Buchanan
出版 :Regnery Publishing,inc.

He well describes the extensive compromises offered by Prime minister Konoye, such as withdrawal from Indo China and the bulk of China. The Japanese wish was that then America would lift the economic embargo. Yet Secretary of State Cordel Hull refused this, he felt that it was not enough. Truly, the Roosevelt administration wanted war.

近衛文麿総理大臣が申し出た対米戦争回避のための妥協案について説明しています。インドシナと中国からの撤退などです。日本が求めていたのはアメリカの経済制裁解除でした。しかし米国務長官のコーデル・ハルがこの妥協案は十分ではないと拒否しました。やはりルーズベルト政権は開戦を望んでいたということがわかります。

John Toland' books

All of his works on WWII are illuminating. They provide a sympathetic view of Japan's war effort.

ジョン・トーランドの第二次世界大戦に関する作品は全て良いものです。彼は日本の戦争に同情的な見方をしています。

◆著者◆

マックス・フォン・シュラー（Max von Schuler）

本名、マックス・フォン・シュラー小林。
元海兵隊・歴史研究家。
ドイツ系アメリカ人。
1974年岩国基地に米軍海兵隊として来日、その後日本、韓国で活動。
退役後、国際キリスト教大学、警備会社、役者として日本で活動。
現在は結婚式牧師、「日出処から」代表講師。
著書に「アメリカ人の本音」（桜の花出版）「太平洋戦争 アメリカに嵌められた日本」（ワック）「アメリカ白人の闇」（桜の花出版）がある。

アメリカ人が語る **アメリカが隠しておきたい日本の歴史**

平成 28 年 11 月 19 日　第 1 刷発行
平成 29 年 8 月 9 日　第 9 刷発行

著　者　マックス・フォン・シュラー
発行者　日高裕明
発　行　株式会社ハート出版

〒171-0014 東京都豊島区池袋 3-9-23
TEL.03(3590)6077　FAX.03(3590)6078
ハート出版ホームページ　http://www.810.co.jp

©Max von Schuler Printed in Japan 2016
定価はカバーに表示してあります。
ISBN978-4-8024-0028-2　C0021
乱丁・落丁本はお取り替えいたします。ただし古書店で購入したものはお取り替えできません。

印刷・中央精版印刷株式会社